We Are Our Ancestors

by

Richard F. Weaver

RoseDog Books
PITTSBURGH, PENNSYLVANIA 15222

ISBN: 978-1-4349-9238-3
Printed in the United States of America

First printing

For more information or to order additional books, please contact:
RoseDog Books
701 Smithfield Street
Third Floor
Pittsburgh, Pennsylvania 15222
U.S.A.
1-800-834-1803
www.rosedogbookstore.com

Forward

This book could be classed as a gift from God. I say that because of an incident in the early morning of the 12ᵗʰ of November 2005, at 2:05AM when I had this weird and very uncomfortable feeling of dying. I had a near death experience or (NDE.) and therefore, would not have been here to tell of what had happened to me. Everything will be explained later on in the book of that experience. During the time I was hovering on the other side of this life, I was shown many of the answers to the reasons of life and why we are here, something which has been largely misunderstood for millennia.

My understanding of what I saw is due to my early studies and research into the religions and ways of the ancient peoples of this world. To have your beliefs substantiated in this way makes you feel very humble indeed. The task I have now is to write down the account of what happened to me and what I saw so that everyone can understand and share in my experience. And also to have a written record for those who will come along in the future in their search for enlightenment and who will be able to benefit from reading it.

It is of great assistance to have some form of guidance in a search of any quest and when there are so few records kept, most of them are by religious groups and are similar in content, the task becomes so much more difficult. Information about reincarnation, spirituality, and so forth are the subjects of my own research, which I found to be one of the most diverse and difficult subjects to find answers to, and when I did find something, what I came across was sometimes evasive and never answered all my questions especially the ones I wanted answers for. Much of what I came across regarding reincarnation* was misleading. It was also confusing and some of it was wrong. Here in this account of my NDE, I hope to solve many of these problems that haunt most people today. The task of writing down what you find out before you pass on is a task which I may have failed to do in my previous life and just in case it was, I have now managed to find the courage that is within me to complete my task here with this following book. I hope it serves you as it was meant to do. The journey you are about to embark on through these pages requires a library type atmosphere of quiet and calm. I sincerely hope you make it to the end.

richardfweaver@hotmail.com

---

*Since completing this book I have found a well balanced book about reincarnation by Dr. Ian Stevenson entitled *Children Who Remember Previous Lives*. This book is too good to miss and is a must.

Introduction

I suppose the build up to my near death experience began in January 2005, when I received a phone call from our long time friends of over forty years, Bill and Pauline. Their request was for me to look out for a Jack Russell puppy in the local newspaper. Sure enough that week there were two dogs and a bitch for sale in Gloucester. I informed them that same evening and they were going to investigate them, if there were none locally in the Bath area where they lived.

Everything was fine with Bill and Pauline; they were both well and looking forward to their quest. The next time we heard from them was in July. Pauline phoned us, she had some bad news. She had been ill and while Bill was looking after her he had collapsed and was taken to hospital. This happened in the June with the very bad news that they had found he had cancer of the stomach. But the big shock was he only had eight months to live.

We wanted to see them as soon as we heard the news and went to see them in early July. It was a sad, but happy, visit which turned out to be the last time I would see him alive. Little did I realise I was having my last beer with him on that precious day. Efforts were made to see each other again, but due to hospital visits and rapid deterioration of health in both Bill and Pauline, this did not occur.

On the 31st of October Bill passed over to the other side and his funeral was arranged for Friday the 11th of November,

Armistice Day, Remembrance Day to all the countless lives lost in the two world wars and all wars since. On Monday that week, I received a bite from one of my dogs. I gave them some chocolate drops and had accidentally dropped a few on the floor when they started to fight over them. I pulled them apart, but got bitten on the hand in doing so. "That bite could kill me," I remarked as I went to clean the wound.

I am not saying that this was the cause of my plight to come, but something had to have started the process off. When I mentioned it to the surgeon doctor who attended me later, he just shrugged his shoulders. I presumed he thought it of no consequence.

Then, three days later on Thursday evening, the 10th of November, the night before the funeral and after taking a bath, I felt a sharp pain in my stomach and groin area as I pressed the towel against it as I dried myself. The pain was quite like colic so I expected it would go away and went to watch television for the rest of the evening. The pain got worse as I sat there, but I thought it would go away after a good night's sleep so I went to bed.

In the morning the pain was still there. I thought it would go after my morning ablutions, but that did not fix it. As I got ready to travel to the funeral the pain never eased up, so my daughter drove the forty miles down to Bath.

The day and funeral passed. Pauline looked very ill indeed, hardly able to complete the day, she suffering from an unknown affliction that the medics had not been able to identify. All through the day the pain in my stomach never eased and it was beginning to worry me, as the pain had been increasing in strength throughout the day. On the trip back home I felt every bump and corner in the road and was very relieved to get home.

At about eight o'clock the phone rang; it was Pauline's daughter telling us that Pauline had died at half past six, just after she had put her to bed. She had arranged all the flowers from Bill's funeral in a display on the patio so that Pauline could see them from her bedroom window and had gone to wake her so she could see them. As soon as she walked into the room she knew her mother had passed from this life.

It really did not come as any surprise, just a shock. Pauline had held out just to complete Bill's send off and now she was where she wanted to be, with him. Life can be so uncertain, in under a year two healthy people had gone from being in full health to their deaths. After I had passed on the sad news to everyone, I decided to go to bed as I was in so much pain. My stomach was so swollen I could not do up my trousers and it seemed going to bed was the best thing to do at the time. Hospital had been mentioned.

As I lay in bed the pain was so bad I could not find a comfortable position to lie in. I was in agony and it followed my every move to alleviate it. Every change of position, each move I made to ease the pain, it came back after only a few seconds. I watched the time go slowly and painfully by; my stomach seemed at bursting point. I had my appendix removed, at the age of eleven, so it could not be that. I suffered for another four hours with no let-up in the severity of the pain and then at just after two o'clock in the morning I was compelled to get up out of bed. I could no longer stand the agony, so I thought if I could relieve myself it may just ease the pain a little, although at the time I did not need or want to go.

As I stood in the small water closet next door to our bedroom, I had the most horrendous feeling of nausea come over me. Then a kind of black swirling came over me like thick fluid, racing around my head, engulfing me. My stomach was churning and convulsing as I staggered back into the bedroom in the most excruciating pain, the black liquid seeming to engulf me completely. Blindly, holding onto the door frame for a moment, I aimed myself towards the bed and shouted to get an ambulance, I am dying. Then I took a huge lunge towards the bed as I was losing all coordination as to where I was and was in fear of losing consciousness. I then sensed I had made it to the bed and heard my wife ask if I really did need an ambulance.

She was about to phone for one when, to my amazement, the pain had eased quite considerably. I told her I was okay, the pain had eased, and I would rest a minute to see how I was. Little did I realise then what had happened to me. I was to find out three days later.

The pain was now bearable and I told my wife I would try to rest until morning and we should take it from there. Now I had a real thick head, no ache, but a heavy thick head. I fell asleep and when I awoke the following morning I felt quite exhausted.

The pain was still there, somewhat easier, but still bad and I still had a thick head. So I stayed there dozing until nine o'clock. I thought it a good idea to stay there all day, but the next moment; I heard a van pull up outside and remembered my nephew was coming to do the electrics on our bungalow so I had to get up. I apologised to him that I could not help in any way as I had a bad gut and could hardly walk, let alone work.

My wife phoned the doctors, but because it was a Saturday there was nobody available and she was diverted to the hospital. She explained the symptoms of my condition and what had happened during the night. They booked an appointment for me and suggested I make my way to them the best I could. They would see me as soon as I arrived and assured my wife I would not have to wait.

During the course of the morning the pain eased to how it was earlier the previous day. I was all for letting it sort itself out, much to the disgust of my wife and also of my daughters, who had arrived to take me to the hospital. "Nothing a good dose of salts wouldn't shift," I remarked, but the tin in the medicine cabinet was rock solid and unusable. I then asked to be taken to the supermarket to get another tin, much to the annoyance and angry comments from my family. As I put on my coat, I had a sharp reminder of the pain and requested the trip should be to the hospital instead. This decision was welcomed and to everyone's relief.

I was admitted into hospital where I underwent the usual examination. An intravenous valve, a cannula, was inserted into the vein in the back of my hand so they could access my bloodstream. I then went to x-ray and finished up in the surgical assessment ward where I had a cocktail of liquids connected to me and I settled down for the night. It was now past midnight.

I was still unaware of the dire predicament I had been in and, in fact, it was not until Monday afternoon when I had had my MRI scan that things started to register with me.

As I lay in the scanner, a blue dye was poured into me via the cannula. The nurse told me that during my scan I would experience a taste in the back of my throat, like iron, then a feeling of relieving myself, or a warm sensation in my groin and I would get a tingling all over. This, I can say, was a pretty accurate description of what occurred in the scanner, only something else happened in there as well. It was the trigger that activated my memory, although I could not quite recollect what it was, because I was bursting to relieve myself, after having had to drink so much water before my scan. It was distracting me from what was stirring in the back of my mind.

I must say that I was very grateful for this strong distraction, because had I started to recall what had happened to me in the early hours of that Saturday morning. It would have caused me to burst into tears of emotion, but because of the urgency of my plight and the fact I was instructed to save all of what I passed for measuring purposes, I was saved from an uncomfortable and embarrassing dilemma. Because while my full attention was with ensuring I returned to the ward with my full urine bottle, having had to plug it with the paper hand towel I had dried my hands with after the event so as not to spill any. The recollections I was to have would not come until later that evening.

As the porter pushed me back to the ward, I dutifully passed my charge to the nurse and was returned to my bed where my wife was waiting for me. It was now thirty minutes into visiting time, 3:30PM. During this visiting time, there were moments of quiet, when the general conversation came to a lull. On these occasions and up until my family had to leave, I was recalling in my mind what had happened to me and some of the things I had been shown, very similar to being in a daydream state.

Consequently, when my wife was about to leave I was very emotional. What she did not know was what I was emotional about. I would be telling her the following day. I had calmed down before she left and assured her I was okay.

I now layback in my bed and recalled the things that had happened to me. The heavy head had emerged again, although it had not really gone away. This was the night of all nights, I did not get a wink of sleep, although I did not want any —I was too engrossed in what I was recalling.

The burst of emotion from me when my wife was about to leave was due to the recall of seeing my funeral and of her having to telephone and tell my daughters that I had died in the early hours of the morning, of the night of Pauline's death and Bills funeral. Here is how it all came to me.

Chapter 1

The first information I received was that I had come to this situation before. I was being informed by what seemed to be a higher being of great wisdom and yet, a being that was part of me, a part in fact of the whole setup. "You were your great-grandfather in your last life, who had died in the Forest of Dean after trying to operate on himself, having had trouble in his groin area."

Wow! This came out of the blue. Nothing was further from my thoughts than my great-grandfather. I had only hearsay information on him, mostly from my now deceased mother and did not even know his Christian name. All I had been told was that he had been the herbalist of the Forest of Dean when my mother noticed I had a copy of a book on herbs and then, at a later time when questions were asked about him, she told me that my uncle, my mother's younger brother, was the person who had found his body in the woods when he was a boy. Later, I discovered my uncle had been eighteen years of age at the time he found him.

The narration went on, "You have reincarnated because of the confusion after your death. Some of your knowledge and beliefs were incorrect and, being alert to the fact, you were anxious to come back and rectify this as soon as you could. To correct that which was of false substance you linked up with your granddaughter for your return to the earth. She was to be your mother."

Wow! Again, I have believed in reincarnation as early as when I was a small child, it seemed a natural thing to happen in my childhood. I was not taught it, it came as a natural thing to me, but this was quite something.

"While the baby was being programmed in the womb, the baby that you were to be, there was an interception into the process to have the programming stopped. There was a claim of priority for the baby to come, from your father-to-be side of the family."

Now the information that I am about to give has never been revealed before. It is one of the reasons why I believe what happened to me to be fact; most of the content is incredible and unbelievable, but not unacceptable. The overriding law, when called upon with regards to reincarnation, came to light when I challenged my adviser as to why I was the second born child, when I had a most urgent need to return to the earth to put things straight and had to wait for the second birth. This was the answer I received.

"The universal laws are made and agreed by everyone when in their true state of spirit; they are the natural laws and are adhered to by everyone while in spirit. Many of these laws are not known in the physical state down on earth and can get broken, the only place they do get broken, but they are generally sensed subconsciously by everyone. Most everybody knows right from wrong. The answer to your question is this that there was a claim made by your father's group family for the baby that you had planned to be. They had someone who needed to return on an urgent task as well, so they used the linage law to achieve this. That universal law is this; the first born child will be a returning soul coming from the father's side. The second born child will be a returning soul coming from the mother's side. This carries on in that order until there is no one ready to return from either family. This may sound contradictory, but if there is no one ready to return from either family group, then it becomes an open slot for anyone who is suited for that life. Of course, your situation is very rare indeed; normally most souls are catered for without any conflict at all, because not that many from a group are ready to return anyway. So, where the two families have an urgent need for a return to the earth, in this case it was both of yours, it's the father or male's family that has the right to the first born child for reincarnation. The mother's family claims the second child. It has always been this way. This is the normal function and process where there is to be a family group continuation, the law is only enforced when there is a dispute. Normally there is no claim and the first born can be from either side, as you yourself were planning this time around, coming from the mother's side. Many times the soul is from a different group altogether, like your father was. There are many times when other spirits can enter from a different group into a different family and individual spirits can choose a family they think will help them evolve more quickly. All this is arranged according to each and every need. These arrangements take place after much deliberation amongst the wise advisors who arrange the placement of the reincarnate who is to return. The advisors, though, only advise, they do not make the final decision as to where you are born, you do. Only you, the returning spirit, can make that decision. We choose who are going to become our parents every time. The only time a spirit is forced back is if that spirit committed suicide in its last life. Then they have got to come back, any other return is decided by the one returning.

While the baby is growing in the womb, all its tasks for its life to come are programmed into the newly growing brain, the probabilities of what will happen in this lifetime, including the opportunity to complete spiritual enlightenment, thus ending the need to return again. This though, requires great effort and is called one pointedness of mind, otherwise it's just another life.

On this particular occasion, your father's group family was in a situation where if they missed this next incarnation, the family group would lose their earthly surname and male link for a return to the earth. Their thinking was that they would have no direct family link back to the earth plane and would have to wait their turn for a suitable host family for their group. This situation is of no importance or consequence to anyone other than the group of your father's family, who thought it important and owing to their state of evolution which had stagnated because in their earthly lives they did not believe in life after death. They had not reached the stage of development either, to accept that the family link did not matter. They had also been the host family for your father's reincarnation, so they thought that this gave them another reason to claim this return.

When your father was born, he was the fourth son and the sixth child of eight children and was not a member of this family group on this return to earth. But he became the only productive producer of children for a possible line linkage for this family, hence his family claim. Lastly, their reincarnating spirit was returning to try and change this family's negative thinking. You had to wait for the next baby to come along, another fourteen months. It is appropriate here to say, each and every soul is an individual, a spirit searching for knowledge. You only belong in a family group for the lessons you can learn from each other until it's time to move on. Those families we join and associate with are for our own convenience; after all, in the end we find out we are all from the same source, just one huge family."

This information brings a dramatic understanding of the tenth and final plague Moses inflicted on the Egyptians, taking the life of the first born child, to free the Israelites from bondage. It makes sense as to why it caused so much more anguish than the other plagues. It's more than probable this law was known at that time, but only by the ruling pharaohs. The consequences of this deed would mean that all the second children, including the concubine children of the Pharaoh, would take priority in the next incarnation coming from the mother's side and leave no direct link for the pharaohs to return and therefore lose their royal linage of return. It should also be noted here that the pharaohs always tried to marry their sisters. This happened in most of the dynasties, according to history. Intermarriage was not uncommon and on occasions the pharaohs even married their daughters. If they became that desperate, there is a suspicion here in my view that they definitely knew of this reincarnation law. They also put the greatest value on their eldest son. This was not only to keep their royal blood line as pure as possible, but to allow them back again.

Moses did them a big favour. He broke the never ending cycle that the pharaohs had got caught up in, (known to some beliefs as the "wheel of life") and were unable to progress their evolution of the soul since they did the same thing each lifetime. The pharaohs kept their people under control by telling them that only they, the pharaohs, could go back and be with the gods after death. Making the people think that the pharaohs were the gods, and they were of little value, unable to have everlasting life, but were in fact the same as the pharaohs.

The similarity to this type of belief has generally been taught throughout the ages by the priests of religion to give them the power over the masses. This has caused a major problem today in the evolution of the soul. We are all stuck in the circle of life. We reincarnate time and time again because we don't have any form of correct teaching to tell us otherwise and most all of us are left with no satisfactory solution to follow. It's no wonder we get trapped into materialism. Believe it or not, Jesus taught us about reincarnation; it was the main structure of his teachings. It gave the masses freedom from the dogmatic power possessing priests who dominated their lives. So what do you think the priests did? Yes, they all got together, had a convention in about the year sixty, and wrote the main theme of their beliefs, making sure they omitted reincarnation and got back complete control.

The moral theme that keeps the church in business is acceptable. But we have had to put up with so much other junk and mumbo jumbo from them over the years which they expect us to accept and believe. We can now challenge their authority, but they think they are the ones that know best. It is now time we questioned their fantasies and progressed. Who in today's modern society actually believes in men with wings? Just because an artist portrays an angel with feathered wings, we are expected to accept this as real or we did when we were children. Everybody knows that men can't fly without some form of assistance, so when the angel of the lord came down and the glory of the lord shone all around, a well used phrase in the Christmas saga, this angel man was assisted by something other than thin air.

Returning to our theme, if you reflect on this newly found reincarnation law and apply it to your own situation, you may find some fascinating and revealing circumstances to which you can relate. But first of all you must remember to take into consideration this fact. If there is no immediate need for a family member to return to the Earth plane in your particular family, then that position is filled automatically by a spirit who is unknown to you.

Someone in your family may not compare in any way whatsoever with you, or the rest of your family. You get on, but you are totally different in every way, or, you may get on so well you are like twins. You may often be drawn to one side of the family more than the other. Then again, you might totally disregard each other and keep your distance; you may even have severed a relationship totally within your family. Whichever way, this should not affect the love you should have for one another, despite your differences, as they say, "blood is thicker than water." In some families you can sense that the eldest child is favoured by the father and the second child is favoured by the mother. I am not saying that either child is less loved, far from it, but you can see a marked trend by their parents who do this subconsciously without realising it and are oblivious to doing it. This can best be observed by the outsider, but sometimes by the children. However, in many family cases where the parents recognise their responsibilities to their children, this rarely occurs.

If you go back only a few generations in your spiritual family tree, rather than tracing your physical name line family tree, you can see how complicated and diverse it gets and you can soon lose track. It is not like the normal surname family tree, although this, in the end, is the typical and general way to trace your ancestors.

With the spiritual family tree, anybody you meet or pass in the street could have been your mother, father, brother, sister, or cousin in a past life. Many of our ancestors are back with us at this time mainly as our children. In turn **we are our ancestors**, and we keep coming back, time after time after time. This makes the mind boggle a bit, but that is the case. One interesting point to make here is that if you were a man last time and gave the women folk a hard time, or vice versa, you will probably come back as the opposite sex next time. There is no license on what sex you come back as, it's a case of what you have come back to learn and what sex would suit the situation best.

It might be useful here to mention how a family group of spirits come together. The most obvious and most usual is through our offspring. Once you have children, you can't get a much greater bond than that, so you follow your loved ones from life to life in a circle. Mostly, there is no one we would rather meet than our own mother when we pass over into the spirit world, or our much loved ones who went before us. But over the many years of our lifetimes, we become attracted to our own kind of people, although we are all individuals in our own right we form into groups of the same thinking minds. In other words, like attracts like; this is another form of group, but still a family group.

When we are living here on this physical world, people who have similar interests discuss them, exploring all aspects of the subject in question. We learn more quickly that way. Sometimes people in the working group have no compatibility whatsoever with the others, but have the same goal in mind, while some are like carbon copies of each other. During these group associations and of course in many other types of meetings, it could happen anywhere, we sometimes find someone who we are on the same wavelength with and find a compatibility and understanding with them beyond our wildest dreams. This is not physical attraction, as some of you may think. When this is very strong, a lifetime bond can be formed and can be a planned reunion from past lives. But this bond is of the type that usually carries on after death and can become the start of another type of learning group, where others join for the same reason. This formed group tries to reincarnate into the same family, as all families do, or as close as possible to the location as to where their loved ones have gone to try and stay together, coming back sometimes as cousins, brothers, sisters, or the nearest relation possible. This then is the makeup of the family groups, the loved ones we meet again on the other side when we leave this world. Then finally, you get the soul who stays aloof from the family, who wishes to stay alone. That is entirely the choice of that soul.

If and when it is time to return and be reborn, the problems we encounter when we return are colossal: the complete losses of our memory, the age gap— we were the adults when we left this earth plane remember, and now we are back, being the children again— the change in the local environment, not everything stays the same. All recollection of the past associations is gone. We have no idea what is going on, instinct and intuition are all we have to rely on, so the odds of finding one another is very difficult, if not impossible. The only sure way, if you could call it that, is to keep it in a family, which is not always possible, but that's how we do it to stay together. The possibility of ever knowing or tracking any of your loved ones in the physical is almost zero. It's never been heard of and if there is any slight recollection of memories in the mind of the new child, if not acted upon or noted when suspected, anything that was there has usually started to fade or has gone by the time the new child has reached the age of three to four years. And unfortunately, this type of thinking is frowned upon and not encouraged by most parents in this present day and age, it is suppressed and this is a very sad state of affairs to be in.

As the family group pools its knowledge and strives to evolve, some of the members may need to enter a different group to get a different outlook. No one is compelled to stay in the group and they can leave at anytime to progress elsewhere. The goal is gaining wisdom, to break the wheel of physical lives, to end all the suffering and pain that can only be experienced down here on earth, and to pass our set tasks so we don't have to come back and start all over again.

As I indicated before, everyone we meet is our distant relation in one way or another. **We are our ancestors**, who have returned to the physical plane, to live out another life. I found out that I was back within only seven years and seven months. Some souls return to the earth even sooner, not spending as much time in the spirit realm as others. The time can vary considerably according to our need. When we return, it is to learn another lesson or lessons. It may be to pay off some debt or you may have returned just to support your family group in the search of enlightenment. It could be that you are a loner, as the saying goes. "You look to no one but yourself for your own salvation," the key to our release.

You can be sure of one thing though: the reason you are back is to learn lessons about everything possible to do with the physical plane of matter and learn to live in harmony with ones fellows. Do this and you will be nurturing and feeding your spirit, your real self. There are things on the physical plane that cannot be learned in the spirit state alone, hence the need to come here. In the world of spirit, there are none of the vices that we have down here on earth. When you are only in spirit on the physical plane remember you pass through solid objects, you cannot touch, speak, or move anything unless under extremely favourable conditions. You can only observe what is happening and then, only if the circumstance allow it. Beware of what you do though, while you are down here on earth living your physical life, because whatever you do will come back to you. You pay for your deeds, either good or bad, and what you cause with your actions has an effect. It is wise to know what you do. The more love you give out, the more you get back. It's the same with the opposite, hate.

The most famous reincarnate, by the way, is the Dalai Lama, the spiritual leader of Tibet. A most interesting process is carried out here, when the time comes, to go and search for his whereabouts, to find out where he has reincarnated. The lengths of effort that go into this are incredible. This also shows how difficult it is to establish a link to a passed life, if the need ever arose. You see, even the Dalai Lama, cannot remember his past lives, but you should be too busy living this life and getting it right to worry about that.

This seems to be a good time to clear up any confusion caused by the misunderstanding of reincarnating into another type of creature. The simple fact is you do not, you cannot. Every different living thing has its own evolutionary path; you cannot come back as a horse, a dog, a cat, a bird, or any other type of animal. The cosmic law will not allow it to happen. We come back as humans, nothing else. So if you say you would like to come back as a bird or something, then you are speaking in jest. It will not happen. The main reason for this misunderstanding is the confusion caused by the interpreter's scribes and priests in the deciphering of the ancient scriptures and manuscripts from the past. They were looking for something mystical in the writings that were not there, trying to glean out every little bit of information, and complicating what is and should be a simple thing with regard to the circle of life. When the priests attended a person who was in the process of dying, giving them certain instructions to follow on their death bed, they would say, "What you have done in this life, will affect what you will be in your next life." The descriptions they most often called upon for describing the characteristics of a certain type of man after he had passed on was that of animals, "He was as brave as a lion," "he was as sly as a fox, as strong as an ox, and so on." These examples were also used to indicate what that person would be like if he or she wasn't mindful when they returned to the earth in their next life. So instead of reincarnating as a mouse, you are reincarnating like a mouse, with the characteristics of a mouse, not as an actual mouse. There is a slight difference in the wording, but a massive difference in the meaning. You can see how easy it is to mix it into the wrong meaning. It is true that all the animals reincarnate. They are evolving the same as we are, but they stay as they are, of what they are, until they have progressed to their spiritual goal.

As animals evolve from this earth, their numbers diminish until they become extinct when they have finished their allotted time here on the earth, unless of course they are needed for the help in keeping the eco system working. Nature is supposed to dictate as to how and when this should happen to them. Unfortunately we, the so called guardians of the animals, most often let them down. Far from being kind and helpful to them, we have caused some to become extinct before they were ready. We ate the dodo, remember? It's time man became responsible for his actions; responsibility is a thing we never take seriously. Man can be so shallow. Some countries are trying their best to rid us of the whale. You would think that the world's largest animal would be safe, especially living in the ocean. It seems the only unendangered species is man. Well, we are slowly destroying our environment, so we too are at risk. It is a thought provoking statement here as to mans makeup: he is the dominant species on this world and he has all the animal characteristics of each and every animal on this world within him. From the most timid and frightened to the most ferocious and brutal, he has no limit he that is man, his cruelty abounds. Only when he is able to subdue and clear his nature of those characteristics can he progress.

Chapter 2

The one thing people don't seem to realise in today's modern world is the fact that we are all linked together in a gigantic web. We are all spirits from the one source moving enmasse through the universe. This was the next thing I was shown in my near death experience. I'll explain how I recall it next.

We are all evolving spirits. Billions and billions of us, like raindrops, all programmed to return to the source. The raindrop tries to return to the ocean. But, in our case, it is to get back to the heavens because we are all part of God, the immeasurable. We are cosmic beings trapped in matter. We are all of the same age, each and every one of us, all on the same journey. We have always been in existence, make no mistake about this. The only difference between us all is that some spirits are more evolved than others. Some are lost, trapped in the material world we have created for ourselves. We are all at different stages of evolution in our journey back; some are more advanced than others. Some have retarded back and have hardly started, and are lost, trapped in their misconception of life. Especially those who do not believe in life after death, reincarnation is well and truly out of their jurisdiction. These negative thoughts stop any form of progress for these souls who have them. They remain in their own limited area of thought and those who have passed over, not aware of life after death, are lost to us and the greater life they deny. They are the ghosts who haunt the areas where they lived, while here on the earth. They are imprisoned in their thoughts of what they think they know and while they are there, in that state of mind, they are unable to be reborn into a physical body, to clean their minds. This state can last hundreds of years.

In Tibet they used to hold a chanting ceremony, calling all the lost souls together to release them. By this organised chanting, a vibration was created that resembled a beacon that attracted all the lost souls in the area to come to that place. The ceremony would then release most of them from the bonds of their negative thoughts which had trapped them, even in the end the most hardened would be released after a few ceremonies. But the mind is all powerful; it is not easy to change it from its set way of thinking. How often do you change your way of thinking?

Emotion is our biggest fault, yet it is one of our assets. We need it, but we need to control it. When we can control our emotions, we gain enlightenment. If we are emotional, all becomes clouded in whatever emotion is experienced at that particular moment. Enlightenment is gained, simply by controlling one's emotions. You can then see and understand things as they really are.

Some souls here on earth are well in advance along the path to enlightenment, but you would have difficulty in telling them apart from the rest of us. In actual fact, you can't tell them apart, they look as normal, as everybody else does good or bad. You can recognise a good soul when you hear them remark, "my conscience wouldn't allow me to do that," when a freak opportunity presents itself to them that is suspect of being wrong to do. We all look the same, but we all don't think the same, so never underestimate your fellow man. You do so at your cost.

It seems inconceivable too, that an advanced soul can regress when reincarnated. It doesn't happen very often because of the work done by the advisors before we come back. But if, as a child, he or she is indoctrinated into a bad system, or brought up in the wrong environment, receives the wrong education and mixes with the wrong people in their early stages of their growing up to adulthood, they can turn out to be a mindless hooligan or even worse. Just imagine how difficult it is for a person to readjust and reform into being a good person. That's what has to happen though and usually to the extreme. They turn out to be born again types and overzealous in their reform trying to balance things out.

That is one of the few problems, if we have any, in reincarnation, but it tests how genuine the soul is and has become. It is up to us to concentrate on the advantages of reincarnation and the wisdom behind giving us all equal chances at the start; to emphasise the importance of being able to come back as a different person, to live another life, so that you don't get categorised and forever condemned is why it's the way it is. An example of what would happen is this: how would a murderer or child molester be able to live and progress if there were no death and he lived forever in a physical body? He would be forever persecuted for his crime and never be able to do anything without hostility. His crime would be his label into eternity. But to come back in a new body, he has a change of identity and nobody knows who he is, not even he does. He now has a chance, first, to put things right and then progress without persecution or recognition to hinder his progress. Extremely bad people are usually extremely good on their return, because the balance has to be made.

The planet Earth is a giant classroom where we come to progress. It is a unique place where the less evolved can be in charge and they usually are. Doesn't that ring true to you in some way? Is that not a massive statement as to why the world is in such a state? The main reason for this is that an evolved soul, rarely seeks fame or fortune, but only tries to do the right thing, or take the right action. The sadness is millions of us have lost our way. We have forgotten our source and from whence we came.

It all started when some of the more adventurous souls wanted to explore the dense physical matter of the universe. And because we are vibrating so fast in the state of spirit, an entire Earth day equals only half a second to the spirit world, we could not touch or feel anything on the physical plane. This was overcome by creating a soft machine (man), consisting of this matter so that we could then get inside it and so reduce our vibrations to the frequency of matter (that is why the Gnostics taught that matter was evil and salvation could only come through knowledge of esoteric spiritual truths). Several types of bodies were tried until we perfected what is now called the human body, able to reproduce itself by gathering up the local elements of matter it required and to use it to build itself. There are many types in use throughout the universe and they are very similar in human likeness to one another, different only from being made up of the matter from their local systems. They also vary in the length of time they live or last. This is governed by the local orbit of their planet around its star, and these soft machines are all allotted the same number of heartbeats, that of two thousand seven hundred million heartbeats, beating at different speeds accordingly, this governs the length of their lifespan on the physical plane keeping them mortal, the soul then returns to immortal spirit.

The model in use on Earth goes through ten progressive growing stages, altering or renewing its molecular structure every seven Earth years, giving it a useable lifetime of seventy Earth years. When they reach this age, they can last longer, but are not as efficient and are of much less use; the body is then discarded by the spirit and returned to the elements it was made from. The spirit that had occupied that body journeys on and can take a rest while reviewing its progress before it decides its future.

These soft machines were widely in use long before the Earth came into being, in other areas of the physical universe. They are the most robust and agile forms for us to use and they have become so good that the spirits, once inside them, think they are the actual life, forgetting from whence they came. Tragically, the ego of the machine takes over. This is a malfunction; it should not happen. They have become faulty. Over the time of continual birth and rebirth, so many of our spirit brothers have become trapped, lost in the illusion that the machine we are inside is the be all and end all of our existence. Nothing can be further from the truth as the physical (machine) body, cannot survive without having a spirit attached to it. Sadly, nothing we have tried to do or have done to rectify this in the past has convinced these disillusioned souls otherwise. The physical human body seems to have developed a mind of its own, ignoring its own spirits existence. Because of it, very few souls are evolving at this present time, so now it has become a serious worry for us. It means that at the present rate of spiritual evolution and evolvement, for this present human race of mankind, especially in regards to the time in which it's going to take for it to happen, the Earth will not last for the duration. So we have a serious problem to overcome: we last forever the Earth will not.

Before the destruction of the Lamastic religious system that was in place in Tibet, there were on average one in a thousand of the monks who gained freedom from the circle of life, they actually evolved. They progressed because of the unique spiritual system that was in place there, prior to 1959 when invasion changed the way of life there. It was of great help to mankind in the quest for enlightenment to have an actual spiritual thinking country, where an evolving spirit from anywhere in the world could reincarnate there to finish off its quest for freedom.

There are records that even Jesus studied there when he was a young man, but alas the country of Tibet no longer exists in that capacity, it has all changed for the worst. Materialism has swept it away, like it did the American Indians. A few countries remain where you might still find food for your soul searching, but they are few in number and are moving away rapidly from the spiritual trend of things. Now you can see how difficult it is going to be for us here in the west to gain spiritual evolution. We are in a materialistic and commercial thinking system, our average for evolving souls will be more like one in a million unless western man can relax, raise his vibrations, and include spiritual progress with material and technological progress, in equal proportions.

We must progress materially, but more so technologically for our development to continue, but not at the cost of our spiritual development. Maybe the American Indians and the Tibetans did not have the right balance and were too much with the spirits for their own good. It makes one wonder, as their technology was in metaphysics and not materialism, so one will never know. Maybe one day, the western world will wake up to the fact that we have all lost a jewel of a country whose sole purpose was to spiritually evolve and their system was unique. I hope in the future this country will be restored to its original status.

I will now describe in the next few paragraphs, the incredible scenes I was shown while in my near death experience. It started with a human body in an upright position, its head had the top of the skull removed so that the brain was exposed and could clearly be seen. All over the brain there were tiny lights sparkling like the ends of fibre optic tubes, or, just as if you were looking up at the Milky Way through a pair of binoculars. The next moment, I could see the earth, with the sparkling brain superimposed upon it. I observed the rotation of the earth and the planets in their orbits. Each time the earth faced a planet, a signal was sent to the brain. It was a wonderful sight. The brain was being influenced by signals coming from the planets at different angles and as they passed, or as a particular point of the earth pointed towards them, like a giant input keyboard of a computer activating the set programs within the human brain. The most signals and activity came from the sun, followed by the moon. I was being shown astrology working its subtle way, controlling the destiny of all of us. I felt so insignificant and marvelled at the massive organisation and display I was being privileged to see and allowed to observe. A massive intelligence was working here in this heavenly setup, far in excess of anything our poor brains here on earth could ever comprehend.

The signals that are coming from the sun, moon, and planets are positive signals that affect our emotions and our destiny. They are mainly prompts that activate our program when the time is due for us to take a particular action. Their subtlety is undetected by us and triggers off preset messages within our makeup during the course of our lives. They can be called instincts; we get an instinct to do or take action about something or other that shapes our course and destiny. Now and again some of these more powerful signals that have less to do with our programs, but are of the influencing kind as to what we do, can be received by us with a double meaning. They can be received in a negative way, particularly if there is a bombardment of them. Our thoughts can then become tarnished if we are not in full control of them; this can create religious fanatics and the like.

The automatic pilot within the brain picks up these signals and converts them into a chemical activity that causes certain mental processes to work. If these signals are received in a negative way, they can manifest as delusions in some way in the thinking of the brain of their receiver. For instance, a person who believes he is doing the right thing in taking other people's lives in the name of religion or at anytime is deluded; his thoughts have been infested and muddled. The same happens when a person seeks revenge if he thinks he's been unfairly treated. He also is deluded, the revenge is the delusion. A person who thinks he has more rights than another is deluded and so on; they are all connected to the ego.

The signals that make us think that way stem from misinterpretations of the signals received by the brain in the first place. The main problem is the reaction of the receiver. A normal thinking and balanced person is not usually affected by these signals in this way. The problem is when a person whose receiver is off balance when receiving these signals starts to make up and amplify these negative thoughts and manifestations in his head and has illusions of grandeur and greatness. He has received the wrong impressions from within himself which caused the delusions in his mind; some even say they have received a message from god. He then amplifies his thoughts, leading him into believing them. The effect is that it boosts his own delusions of greatness and grandeur which fills him with false values. These niggling signals have to be overcome by us all in the course of our progress upwards and have to be discarded by the wayside with the bad thoughts that go with them and be suppressed, if possible, at all times. If you allow them to cross the fine line, you become unbalanced and, because of our free will, they can have dour consequences for us.

This has caused major misunderstandings in this world in the past; a slight deviation or an interruption of a signal can change an entire event if the person who has received these signals is in a responsible position of authority. The subtleties are immense, with horrifying consequences; you can see some of the results by looking at an example of the country of Zimbabwe with Robert Mugabe, and before that Uganda with Udi Amin. There are many more who could be mentioned that were affected by the unfortunate name of lunacy where their balance of reception is overshadowed by their over inflated egos.

The Earth is a negative world at the moment, so the negative forces are much stronger and received much easier than the positive ones. All the more reason for you to be as positive as you possibly can to help restore the balance and bring harmony to our poor old world. There are too many lunatics here on earth at the moment who are so easily influenced by the moon. They give the moon a bad name because it's not only the moon that has this effect, the sun and planets have as much influence. Even the distant stars of the constellations can upset the individual. So control your body and thoughts like you do when you drive and control your car. Astrology affects the macrocosm as well as the microcosm in exactly the same way.

I will take a slight deviation from our present theme to comment on the way western astrology has been incomplete over the years of development. It may be of interest to you here so you will be able to see how hit and miss the general astrologers are and how it attracts skeptical criticism of astrology itself by astronomers and scientists who target the forecasters in the daily newspapers etc. Their biggest cause of error, and that of most astrologers, is the fact they do not include the most important day of your life: the day of your conception. On and around two weeks either side of this day is the most positive time of the year for you. It is because you had on this day decided to make a link back to the physical world and return to the Earth for a new life, a very positive decision for you to make. After six months of developing in the womb, halfway through the year, and two-thirds through your baby growth, you get to your most negative day of the year; the opposite month to your conception day month. As you start approaching your birthday and onwards from your birthday to your conception day, you become more positive. We wax and we wane throughout the year just like the moon waxes and wanes when it goes through these phases during her orbit around the Earth. It is all a very subtle thing, indeed, and you would not normally notice any difference to your being unless you were hypersensitive. The older you get, though, the more obvious it becomes. All you have to do is check it out on your own life, you will find that the most successful events in your life take place in and around the date of your conception, which is on average ninety nine days after your birth date, give or take a week or two. The most difficult times occur in and around your most negative day, the opposite side of the year to your conception date. As you go through life, you can control your destiny if you give yourself a little time to consider the time of the year it is before you make a decision or when you decide anything. So if it is nearer to the negative day, you should give extra thought and planning to your decision, on what it will be or what you should do. Your instincts and your conscience are your true guide in this, so listen to it carefully so you have the right feelings. Be careful not to allow blind ambition to influence any major decisions. In this way, you can save yourself from all manner of unnecessary problems which come from bad decisions; you hold your own destiny in your hands and you should control it. Don't rely on others to do it for you, especially the forecasters of any of the daily newspapers.

We are cosmic beings and are affected by the cosmos, whether we like it or not. Just to show you how organised the main players are in our solar system, consider this: the sun takes twenty-six Earth days to rotate, plus two days and a bit to catch up with the Earth's position in its orbit around it, making it just over twenty-eight days- the same time as the female menstrual cycle. The moon takes the same amount of time, just over twenty-eight days to orbit the earth, that's why she is called the maternal mother and governs most life on Earth. So the moon and the sun are very closely linked in their coordination and position in regards to their movements, as they are both in nearly the same aspects with one another every day, progressing with a slight difference to each other during the month so as to make each of the twenty-eight days a little different. This means that on every day of the moon cycle, starting from the day of the new moon, the same place and position of the sun's face that was pointing towards the moon on the previous new moon is the same. They are in unison with each other so each day has a sun/moon (father/mother) meaning.

A curious thought here, if the year was arranged to be a lunar year with thirteen lunar months of twenty-eight days equalling 364 days, instead of the twelve months, 365 day calendar year, you would be able to predict the weather with a little more accuracy than can be forecast by the weathermen with all the modern equipment they have today. With today's modern calendar, all is in confusion because the lunar year doesn't tie in with the modern Earth orbital calendar of 365 days. There is no coordination with the days of the previous year, so no day can be compared. But if you compare the days of the lunar year, where you can get similar days in relation to the moon's phases, you can get a much better idea as to how the weather will be. For example, the last week of the four week lunar cycle is almost always the best. I have noticed over the years that the finest, sunniest days happen most often on the day before the new moon, although it is obvious that there are rain clouds in the atmosphere all the time and it can rain where these clouds are, this observation still runs true. So if you could change to, or incorporate, a lunar calendar and say that the last day of every month is most likely to be a fine and sunny one and the likelihood of all the lunar days being similar where they coincide, what an advantage that would be. Now you know why the eastern countries start their new year on the day of the new moon; their days fall almost the same every year. We would be better off with a thorough investigation into the workings and mysteries of the solar system. We haven't even touched the surface yet, but the astronomers rule and they don't prescribe to astrology. With that train of thought, the slight deviation ends here. Let's get back to our theme.

Everything is in a state of vibration, otherwise it cannot exist. We have a positive side and a negative side, just like a battery. One side is white, one side is black and each side has an equal amount of the other. The black side is half white and the white side is half black, so no one can ever say all is bad or all is good. We are equal and even when we are born, we can become either good or bad in our lives, that is up to each of us. Your conscience is your guide, always apply it to everything in your life, and never turn it off. If you do, you become a mindless thug capable of doing anything evil, and mindless action is the cost which you have to pay for in the end, known as the law of karma. Be warned, taking hallucinatory drugs or getting blind drunk can and will turn off your conscience. It also drives your spirit out from the body, although you still remain connected to it; it takes place when you don't know what you are doing and your actions become unknown to you. You are still held completely responsible for them and you pay for them as if you had made them knowingly.

The brain is a soft computer. It has to be programmed to do the tasks at hand. If your computer is lacking a certain program, it cannot do the things of that program. Just like your brain sometimes cannot understand a certain thing, you have to program yourself. *Educate* yourself to that which is to your need. Unfortunately, the time we are best programmed is when we are children. If the program is faulty or inaccurate when it is administered, then we have problems later in life. We rely on what we were taught. This means we are conditioned into the system we live in and if something, such as what I am revealing here, doesn't conform to the system we know, then the natural thing for the brain to do is to reject it. Please don't do that, try and understand, discriminate with the bits that you know and have heard to be correct and let your conscience be your guide. Some parts might be familiar to you and other parts should feel right, even if you can't believe it. People do not have to believe, nor do they have to disbelieve. All that is required is an open mind and a desire to investigate without being biased, you will be better off for doing this. We are unfortunately indoctrinated with false values as well as being misinformed on many subjects when we are in our childhood and this has to be overcome before we are able to progress.

Now the problem with a computer is it will only do what you tell it to do. Then when you get it up and running, you go onto the Internet to gain information and knowledge and you pick up a virus. It messes up your programs and your computer has to be rebooted to try and fix it. Sometimes you cannot get rid of the virus unless you take drastic action and format your hard drive and start all over again. When you do that, all the information and memory you had stored on it is lost, gone forever. Only you, the operator, know what was contained in the memory.

This is just like the brain, but it takes a bit more time. You as an individual are born; you grow up, and during that process adventure out; go into the environment, out into the big wide world, and pick up information. Some is positive, some is negative; it comes to you in the way your brain interprets it. At the end of your life, you have gained a wealth of knowledge and stored it in your mind. All the useful stuff is retained by the mind or, in this case, you the operator. So when you die your brain, in a way, gets formatted and all it contained that is of any use is retained by you, the operator, the person who used that brain and body. When you are reborn the new brain you will own, along with your new body, will have no information or programs on it to start with, only the self maintenance survival program that comes with the body, the automatic pilot so to speak, that works the breathing, digestion and body functions etc.

It takes a baby about two years to find out how to work its body, as there are no instructions on how to work it. So when you come back to the earth you have no memory, or very little, of what you left behind with the operator, the being of your subconscious in that life. You have to start all over from scratch and the frightening thing for all of us is that there is no guarantee that we will find our way when we get here. There are so many distractions and pitfalls put in our way, it becomes a mammoth task. Most of the distractions are trivial, meaningless stuff, placed before us just to entertain us and keep our minds occupied, diverting it away from the real goal. We enjoy the easy, entertaining illusions that are placed before us. It satisfies our needs, so we think, but we delude ourselves. Most of it is useless to us, no good whatsoever. The trouble is, our mind never sleeps. It needs constant entertainment, otherwise it gets bored; we get bored, so we fill it with junk, just for a quiet life. It is laziness on our part. What good is a head full of information on, say football history about teams and players, or a whole load of pop star names? Or who played the part of James Bond in *Dr. No*, etc.; this includes all trivia and there's oodles of the stuff. When we die, all we can take with us on our journey to the other side is what we have acquired in knowledge and experience, nothing else. It is up to us to investigate our being. It's the most important thing we will ever do.

Ask yourself this question: why am I me? It is a simple question, but hard to answer. I asked myself this question when I was in my teens, when I wasn't satisfied with anything I knew or had been taught at that particular time in my life. I realised then that all and everything I knew about didn't answer these inquiring questions about myself, the ones I wanted answers to. Then another question came to me: why am I not somebody else? Then another question: why am I not that person standing over there? Or that person stood there? And back to *why am I me*? I am insignificant, unimportant, ordinary, and plain. I am just a layman of no consequence, just like millions of other plain old me's. Why can't I be somebody else? But that's just it; I cannot ever be anyone else. I am me, always will be me, and nobody else but me. Neither can you, the reader, be any different. It's the individuality, the divine spark of life, that we all are and possess. We might wish to be somebody else, but that's as far as it goes. We can pretend to be someone else, like hundreds want to be Elvis Presley, but they are not, they are themselves. Even when Elvis Presley is reincarnated, he still would not be Elvis Presley, not anymore. He has a new life, one more life to add to his collection. He might even think when he is about eighteen years of age, *why am I a plain old me? I wish I was somebody famous*, like we all do at some time when we are young, we think we have to be a somebody, but that's all one big con to divert you. Trying to be unique, trying to be different because we think we are the same as everybody else, well now you know you are unique, there is nobody else like you, and so you can now get on and spiritually evolve. Do to others only kind things in your actions, treat them how you would want them to treat you. This is life's ideal code for everyone to put into practice along with a bit of harmony and plenty of humour as well, to make your journey a little smoother along the road to home.

I must say here that I have no recollection whatsoever of my past life. It is also important to know that this is how it was meant to be. This also includes almost everyone else born on this earth; no one knows who they were last time. I have no desire to know much about it anyway. As I have said before, people can waste a lifetime trying to find out what they did in a past life when they should be living the one they have now. But a little time spent investigating your family tree, which is a different matter, can be revealing and also refreshing as long as it does not become an obsession that would take up all of your time.

Chapter 3

The nurse on night duty stirred into action; it was 5:30 in the morning. I had been awake all night recalling all that had happened to me in my near death experience. I was a little concerned, no, I was very concerned that what I had been told and shown was very controversial and was also of great significance to all of us down here on the physical world, the Earth, where we are living most of our lives so meaninglessly. That is not meant in a hurtful way, just a wakeup call to promote a soul search to analyse ones outlook and to question ones motivation.

No doubt it will be difficult for me to explain, although I had understood most of what I saw. So maybe it will be difficult for some people to understand, but that will be their challenge. So it is up to me to try and put it into the words that make it easy reading for everyone and to make it as understandable as possible and hopefully, it will be helpful to the majority who come across it. The reason I say this is because I found that when I was receiving this information, my awareness increased by an enormous amount. Not only did it seem that I was aware of all that was happening around me, but I was understanding it without any problems. To me it was flowing so easily it was like a stroll in the park, but now back in the lower vibration of our physical world it has become somewhat of a difficulty, like hard labour or a heavy burden, to try and put into words some of the things that have never been explained before. Regardless of this, I will do my best.

So, what I had to think about first of all was, did it really happen and will anybody believe me when I tell of my experience? The answer to the first question is yes, I think it did happen. As I stated in the introduction, information that had never been available before had materialised from this experience. On the second point, maybe I will just have to take that chance; if I don't write it down, nobody will know anyway. The frightening prospect of telling my story did not appeal to me one bit and gave me cause for concern.

As I lay there in my hospital bed, during this early quiet period of the morning, I was now able to periodically contemplate the wealth of information I was given. Then I had the thought, my eldest daughter was coming to visit me at lunch time and the question was: should I tell her of my experience? Or should I forget the whole thing? I became apprehensive and I can tell you this was a very agonising decision I was going to have to make and I was heading strongly in favour of the latter. This indeed was what I had decided to do, after churning it over and over in my mind, it was for the best. To save any embarrassment, I would keep it all to myself and lock it away in my memory bank out of the way; nobody would be any the wiser and things would stay as normal. But this was the wrong decision because I was still anxious, still uneasy; I had made a final decision and should be contented, but I wasn't. I could not relax and remained on edge, fidgeting and getting hot and then going cold.

As I lay there trying to get into a quiet calm, my thoughts progressed to the time of my death. I had been my great grandfather the last time around and I had come to this situation before. This went over and over in my mind; I came to this decision before, the decision? There was some message; it was trying to tell me something. Then I got it, I remembered the incident in my near death experience, the impression in my head. The voice told me, "You have arrived at this situation before, you have come to it again and you had failed to pass on what you had learned in your last life. You now have the opportunity to go back to your present life and rectify this for the benefit of others by revealing it to all, that's what you should do. Otherwise this cycle you are in will continue and all this trouble and effort will have been for nothing and pointless. And sadly there will be no reason for you to go back! The **decision** is yours and only yours."

I was promptly shown my funeral to emphasize the point. I felt like I was doing a deal with my guardian angel, my over-soul, it was important and essential that I return. The emotional trauma and anguish that would engulf my family if I didn't return would be too much for them to bear, not to mention what effect it would have on me. And the effort made by my kindred spirits, when they suspended me in time to keep me on the borderline between life and death, this took an enormous amount of effort on their behalf; that would have been wasted. I felt the presence of both Bill and Pauline on that fateful night three days ago and this seemed to be the reason for their passing so close and so quickly, to help keep me here for this task. I do not know how much effort was put into that incident or what the spirits did to me on that very early morning, but the result is that I am still living here on earth; I live to tell the tale, so to speak.

This then was what I came back to do, to tell what I know. There's no doubt in my mind now about that and I'll have to face the consequences. It is much better than not being here and having a load of unfinished business. Although my decision early that morning was a negative one, that of me choosing the easy way out of taking no action, the truth was I had a task to do. This task was to inform my family and others of what I know and of my experience of what I saw. I was to reveal all, so I would be telling my daughter when she visited me this lunchtime after all.

After I had made that decision, everything seemed to go like clockwork. It was uncanny. I was able to sleep for a while, maybe two hours, before my daughter arrived and she was an hour early. I had plenty of time to tell her about my experience and with no interruptions to break my concentration. The outcome of that visit resulted in my daughter obtaining the inspiration to design the front cover of this book, my thanks to you Mrs. Karen Cole., for a splendid creation.

After spending just over a week in the hospital, I was allowed to go home. I had to take a course of antibiotic tablets, but otherwise I was okay. It was thought that I had had a cyst or something on the wall of my small intestine which had leaked into my body, as it showed up on the x-ray as a dark area surrounded with whitish patches indicating a leak of some kind. I was also tested for other ailments, including cancer, but thankfully I was clear. The doctors used some technical jargon to explain what they thought I had, but the words were so long I could never repeat them even if I tried. I will stick with the simple stuff, it makes more sense.

It seemed only right to follow up the information of me being my great-grandfather by investigating who he was, but I had no idea where to start. So first, I went onto the Internet under ancestry and typed in my grandfather's name on my mother's side, Frank Trigg, and found a link to a Tom Trigg. I now had a name to work on.

The small amount of information that I already had was gathered from my now deceased mother. She had told me that my great-grandfather (her granddad), had been the Forest of Dean herbalist. This had interested me at the time she told me and I wondered then if he had ever kept a record of the herbs and what they were for. I convinced myself that he had. But she also told me that he tried to do an operation on himself for a rupture or something in his groin area while out in the woods and had died there at that location.

My uncle, Mother's younger brother, used to go on long walks with him looking for herbs, right from when he was a young boy. He was the one who had eventually found him; she said that he was just a boy when he found him, but this turned out to be incorrect and was the cause of my own misinterpretation. I had falsely presumed from my mother's words "only a boy" was how my uncle was when he found him. I was incorrect in thinking this; in fact, he was eighteen years of age when he found my great-grandfather. This though, I wouldn't find out until later and was the reason for a prolonged search for the facts.

The last disturbing thing my mother told me about the incident was that a lot of people thought he had committed suicide. She had heard this from the usual gossip that follows such an event. I must say I was very unhappy with that accusation because of all the crimes one can commit against oneself, suicide is the most serious and the most harmful. It is the worst thing you can do to yourself. You are destroying the temple of your soul; although it is only a shell, it is the most valuable thing you will ever own on this physical world. Without it, you cannot progress here.

I built a picture up in my mind of his notebooks, with all his records about herbs in them, being burnt. I presumed this was because no one had seen them or even heard of these books. But the fact is things were very rarely written down in those days, everything was by word of mouth. So there were no notebooks. This was because he never did write any of it down, it was all kept up in his head. This is the reason why so much knowledge is lost and why it is so important to pass on what you know. These presumed thoughts of mine, about book records and how I imagined him, was a warning to me to be careful not to mix my own thoughts in with my near death experience.

As I recall going back, the scene I was allowed to see was at the very end of my last life. I only saw, or should I say, felt myself trying to get back into an old body. I was floating above this curled up body and feeling warm and free, after being so cold and alone, but I also had a feeling of despair (see appendix). I had a feeling of absolute despair at not being able to finish off or complete any of those tasks that should have been finished off. *"Never put off until tomorrow, what you can easily do today."* This feeling is comparable to a time when you are awakened from a deep sleep. Halfway through a long, really enjoyable dream, you awake when something interrupts and disturbs you, then you are unable to go back and finish it off. You try to remember where you got to, but try as you might you just can't get back. Nothing is more frustrating and annoying than this, only we are talking about our life here, not a dream. That's what it feels like when you have unfinished business; only it's ten times worse when you die than when it's only a dream. It is a stark warning for us all to finish things off and complete all actions if we can before we die.

The next stage of my investigation took me to the Gloucestershire record office to look for birth and death dates. I had no idea when my great grandfather had died or that of his birthday, but by erroneously thinking my uncle was only a boy when he found him I began my search from 1923; my uncle would have been six years of age then. There was no record of Tom Trigg in any of the years from 1923 to 1929, for good measure I included from 1920 up to 1929. After four visits and still no further forward, I decided to go through all the recorded deaths throughout the whole country until I got a result. This sounds dramatic, but wasn't that difficult. I only had to check on one name and that was Tom Trigg.

There were four microfilm cards for each year, so I was a little while searching. Then, I found a Thomas Trigg who died 26th of June, 1930. This date was three days after my birthday and I thought I was on to something. It is quite a normal reaction to look for a possible link by dates to a passed life; there is usually some indication or sign of some sort or another. I transferred from looking at the microfilm to the newspaper records and duly found a Thomas Trigg from Drybrook. He was admitted into Gloucester Royal Hospital on the 25th of June for an operation, but died from a heart attack the following day after undergoing a successful operation. This could not possibly be my great-grandfather, just my luck that there were two Thomas Triggs in Drybrook, so as it was, back to the microfilm.

It took another trip to get what I was looking for. I finally found a Tom Trigg registered dying between October November December 1935; the only one, curiously enough, that I had came across. All the others were Thomas. I still had doubts in my mind because the year of his death, that of 1935, seemed much later than I was thinking. This was twelve years in excess of what I led myself to believe and would only leave me with less than eight years in spirit before my return in June 1943. I quickly transferred to the newspaper records in anticipation. There was bound to be something in the papers about someone dying in the forest, especially under the circumstances. To my dismay someone had managed to put the film with the three months I needed to look at backwards on the film reel, so I would need a mirror to read the film because it projected back to front. I had almost run out of time before the office closed, so I decided to come back again another day.

On my return a week later, I duly took out the film and put it in the viewer. Alas, it was still the wrong way around and nobody had viewed it to correct it as I had hoped. So I took it upon myself to correct it, twisting the film over then slowly and manually winding it onto another spool. It worked brilliant, now for the search; slowly going through for October photo page by photo page. I found nothing; then on into November. I got to Armistice Day, then a bit further and then bingo! I was now about to read what had been kept quiet by my family all those years ago, all those years of silence, criminal silence, so unnecessary silence; I had arrived at my goal. Here it was, *The Citizen*, Wednesday November 20th 1935, headline: Drybrook man's death in woods. Missed by search party. Inquest verdict. The following italicised words are the newspapers actual reports from 1935 in full, as I copied them from the photocopies I made.

Inquest verdict? This meant that there was no report of the incident in the paper in the first instant, so I would have to back track to make sure, but here in full is what I first read.

It was stated at the Forest of Dean inquest yesterday that a man, whose body was found in a wood near his home, would not have died if a party had succeeded in their search for him the previous night.

The inquest, conducted by Mr. M. F. Carter, was on Tom Trigg (74), of Drybrook, and the verdict was death from exposure and loss of blood following a self-inflicted wound in the left groin caused by a razor.

Cecil G. Trigg, of Drybrook, said his father, who had worked for 52 years as a miner, had lately occupied himself with gardening and hairdressing. He had been healthy and active. He used to walk miles every day, but when he did not return home on Saturday the relatives became concerned. A search party set out to scour the surrounding woods and they continued till 3 a.m. without result.

Frank Trigg, [my granddad,] *of Hazel Hill, Drybrook, another son, said his father seemed strange and depressed on Saturday morning.*

Wound Two Inches Long

D. H. H. Sumption said Trigg had a wound in the groin about two inches long. "I think the loss of blood caused him to faint." The doctor said, and he died from exposure. If he had been found before he would no doubt have lived because he had missed the main artery.

P. C. A. W. Johnson said he helped to search the woods on Saturday night. It was reported to him just after 1.o'clock on Sunday that the body had been found. He went to the place and saw the body. There was a blood-stained razor in the case in the jacket pocket and a walking stick and cap some distance away. Twenty-five minutes walk from the place where the body was found, there was indications that Trigg had fallen forward to the ground.

"He had always spoken to me" the constable said, "but for the last two weeks he had passed me by. He did not seem to notice me or anything."

Well, well, I was now hungry for more, so I filed the film back and moved onto the *Journal*, the weekend paper. I whizzed through to Saturday 23rd of November, 1935, *Gloucester Journals*, headline "Drybrook Man's Death in Wood." As I read through it, I realised it was exactly the same report and also noticed that it didn't quite make sense. That is typical of the press, even in those days they had cut the report down in size to fit the column as I found out later. I then thought surely there must be more. I scanned the other film again to see if there was another report of the incident before the inquest report, not a thing; I had come to a halt. I idly continued sifting through the pages then I found more, on Friday November 22nd, the headline read, "Found Dead in Wood. Drybrook Funeral of Mr. T. Trigg." Maybe this article would give me more information:

The funeral of Mr. Tom Trigg (74), of Drybrook, who was found dead in a wood near his home following a two days' search by villagers, took place yesterday.

A native of the district, Mr. Trigg was married about 53 years ago, and there were five sons and two daughters of the marriage, and 24 grandchildren and five great grandchildren. Mr. Trigg had worked for 52 years as a miner, and had been employed in the Severn Tunnel while tunnelling was in progress. Well-known as a local herbalist, he had for some 50 years been the village hairdresser, and for 40 years he was a member of the Drybrook Congregational Men's Bible Class.

Before the cortege left the house a large gathering of friends sang, "Jesu, Lover of My Soul," Mr. J. Bower reading the verses and leading the singing. The cortege proceeded to Holy Trinity Church, where the services in the church and at the graveside were conducted by the Rev. S. E. Easter (vicar).

The mourners were many, too many to list and would be of little interest, only at the end of the list it mentions, *and many others, including members of the Congregational Church, members of the Drybrook Women's Labour party and the Drybrook Women's Institute.* It seems the whole village turned out for him. I searched a few more pages in the hope of seeing more, but to no avail, so that was about it. I spun the film back and thought there was another local paper I could remember my granddad used to read called the *Forest Mercury*, and there should be a better report in that. When I enquired at the record office reception, I was told they kept those records at Cinderford Library, so that was my proposed next stop. I couldn't help thinking though, that there must be more. Why did he cut himself open with a razor? There must have been a reason; something was playing on his mind for up to two weeks before that fateful day. Surely they would have examined the body to find out why he did what he did to himself, to see what was troubling him at the time and to grant peace of mind for the family.

I arranged to call at the Cinderford Library after lunch, from 2:00 to 2:30PM: due to the constant booking of the projector viewer this was the only half hour slot available before a fully booked afternoon. Otherwise it was usually available after six o'clock on the late evenings. My wife and I arrived during lunchtime, waited for the opening, and then proceeded to the viewer. The thirty minutes seemed to race by and eventually we found something. In our panic to get information, due to the time running out on the booked viewer, we hastily photocopied the article and left to read it properly at home. This is what we read:

Dean Forest Mercury, Nov 22ⁿᵈ the late Mr. T. Trigg. Headline: *Big Attendance at Drybrook Funeral. The funeral took place at Holy Trinity Church yesterday (Thursday) of Mr. Tom Trigg who met his death under tragic circumstances on Saturday last. (The report of the inquest appears on page six). Mr. Trigg who was 74 was very well known. He was a native of the Forest and married Miss E. Roberts of Mitcheldean, some 53 years ago. They had five sons and two daughters. Three of the sons and the two daughters live in the district, one son resides at Blackwood, and one at Hemel Hempstead, London. Mr. Trigg had worked 52 years as a miner; he had worked in the Severn Tunnel whilst it was being tunnelled. He attended the Congregational Church regularly till his death. For 40 years he was a member of the Congregational Men's Bible Class. He was well known as a local herbalist, and for many years was the village hairdresser. Late Saturday last, when it became known that he was missing, a large number of villagers immediately came forward and a search party went out until the early hours of Sunday morning and again on Sunday.*

It went on to say about the friends singing before the funeral and the mourners, the same as the report before. Because it was a very bad, blotchy, and faded photocopy, I had difficulty reading it and I must say I was disheartened that there was nothing more. It wasn't until later that evening I realised there was something different about that report, so I picked it up and reread it again. There it was in brackets, "*the report of the inquest appears on page six.*" In our rush to vacate the viewer we had had no time for a thorough search and had missed page six, or a horrible thought, it was missing.

I telephoned the library the next morning and asked them if they would kindly search the film for me at their convenience and let me know if there was a page six on the film and any of the information I had been looking for. I must say the service was excellent, yes there was a page six containing the full inquest. I returned to review and photocopy the film on the late evening opening shift. Here is the last and final information I was able to get. I will print it in full, even though some of it is the same or similar, it is easier to understand and more logical as it is the complete report with no mistakes:

Death from Exposure. Man found Injured after All-Night Search.

Inquest at Drybrook. On Tuesday afternoon the Divisional Coroner (Mr. M. F. Carter) held an enquiry at the police station at Drybrook concerning the sad death of an old and respected inhabitant, Tom Trigg, who had worked in the local mines for over half a century.

Witness Cecil Garnett Trigg, Drybrook, son of the deceased, said "his father was 74 years old and had been a miner, and he had lived near him. He saw him most days. His father was much quieter lately, but, for his age he was in fairly good health and was active he was fond of walking, some days for miles. On Saturday, he told my mother that he was going out for a walk-she understood his usual walk. Towards tea time they became concerned about him, and a search was started. This continued till about three o'clock on Sunday morning. I was one of the search party, with P. C. Johnson. About one p.m. on Sunday afternoon, on a second search, they found him in the Meend enclosure at the Stenders. He was not a long way off the main track through the enclosure. He was lying on his right side, and they found he was dead. P. C. Johnson was notified, and he went to the spot. He was under the impression that he was suffering from a rupture. He had not complained to me about that more lately. He seemed, however, lately, to worry much over little things which did not concern him. He had never made any threat whatever about taking his life and he had never been attended for mental depression or anything like that. He complained of giddiness, and that might have worried him too, but there was nothing apart from that. He had been able to eat well, and had his breakfast on Saturday morning as usual. To my knowledge he slept well. He had worked underground for 52 years. He had done odd jobs of gardening, etc., in recent years." This ended Cecil Triggs statement.

P. C. A. W. Johnson, Drybrook, said "the fact of deceased being missing was reported to him, and he telephoned to a son at Blackwood [Percy Trigg], *where they thought he might have gone, and circulated his description to the adjoining police stations. Later the same night about a dozen of them searched the woods, with no result. At 1.10 p.m. on Sunday afternoon, it was reported to him that he had been found. He went to the spot and found him lying on his right side in a doubled-up position, his knees drawn up. He turned him over on his back and saw his trousers were unfastened. His shirt was saturated with blood. There was a wound in the groin, and they searched about for a knife or some other instrument, but failed to find anything.*

With help, he conveyed him to his son's home and called for Dr. Sumption. On examination the doctor stated there was a cut. A blood-stained razor, in its case, was found in one of his pockets. He had been found 25 paces from the main path, and his hat and stick were near. It was about 25 minutes' walk for him from his house. P. C. Johnson could say that for about a fortnight he had appeared very depressed. He had not seemed to speak to him or anyone else as he passed. He had been out about 24 hours when he was found. It was a very wet night, and they had searched over where he was found, but they had not seen him then." This ended his statement.

Frank Trigg [my granddad and son!], *Hazel Hill, Drybrook, said "he last saw deceased alive on Saturday morning at about 11 o'clock, near the Police Station, Drybrook. "I was on duty at the Social Service building and saw him through the window, concluding that he was, as usual, going for a walk. He had last previously spoken to him on Thursday. He was at my home, and then seemed very strange at intervals, and appeared very depressed."* This ended his statement.

Dr. H. H. Sumption stated that he had known deceased for ten years. He used to see him about twice a year previously.

He had a double hydrocele. Except for that, he did not think he had ever attended him. He was without pain, and therefore he did not think it worried him. About two years ago he saw Mr. Alcock at Gloucester, to see whether there should be an operation, but he did not favour it.

"I was called and saw him on Sunday and found a wound one and a half inches to two inches long, gaping, about one and a half inches wide, deeper on the inner side and superficial on the other side, missing the principal, or femory, vein, but cutting some small veins. I came to the conclusion that the loss of blood caused him to faint, and he died from exposure. He had time to put the razor back into the case." The injury was consistent with having been caused by a razor: the primary cause of death was exposure and loss of blood. He thought he had been trying to cut the vessels, but he did not know quite where they were. This ended the doctor's statement.

The Coroner said under those circumstances it was not necessary to inquire into his state of mind, and he found a verdict that he died from exposure and loss of blood following the wound in the left groin. It was a very sad circumstance that, after such a wonderful record, he should come to his end in such an untimely way.

End of inquest. So there you have it, all I could find out about my great-grandfather, the poor man.

I can't help but think by reading that, he was fated not to be found. There was certainly something playing on his mind over the last couple of weeks of his life. Trust him to do it on the day of a wet and cold November night. The doctor said he had a *"wound one and a half inches to two inches long, gaping, about one and a half inches wide, deeper on the inner side and superficial on the other side, missing the principal, or femory, vein."* It was deeper on the inner side, this tells me that he had probably taken or cut something out of his groin area, as this would leave a wound larger on the inside, which is what was found. If this had happened nowadays we would have had a thorough search of the area and maybe they would have found whatever it may have been that he removed from his groin. Alas, we will never know what happened, although I am now confident and satisfied that it was not suicide as many of the family were lead to believe at the time and in which they never tried to clear up, but left it as it was, a mystery never to be talked about again. I draw my conclusion from the fact that the easiest and most obvious thing for him to have done if he wanted to commit suicide, was for him to have slashed his wrists with the razor he had in his pocket. This shows any reasonable thinking person that he had no intention whatsoever of committing suicide.

So at least we have a date for his death, Saturday, the 16th of November, 1935. Seventy years almost to the day that I had my near death experience. This was on the Saturday the 12th of November, 2005. Was this a coincidence or what? The excruciating pain I had in my left groin that caused it all coinciding with the operation he carried out on himself. That the memory took three days to manifest after the M. R. I. scan also closes the time difference, so you are talking as near as you can get to the day. Was I speculating or is that close? And in my own situation my friend Bill had died two weeks before, bringing me sadness and concern for two weeks prior to my plight. Maybe I'm speculating a little bit, but it does seem to tie in somewhat.

I am trying, logically, to tie the links and facts together, to make some sort of sense out of it all. Did my great-grandfather die in the early hours of the Sunday morning, about the same time of the day it happened to me, roughly 2 o'clock in the morning? We will never know, but it would make sense if he had. They say the body reaches its lowest ebb at 2:00AM., during the hours of darkness, the time when most people die. The report said he would have survived if they had found him on the first search. What I am saying is, we should look for even the smallest of signs in this kind of situation, in regard to reincarnation, or we will never be able to find a link to our obvious past lives. There will always be some form of guide, its finding what kind of guide they send you, or what's already here now. Use your sixth sense, we all possess it, it just lies dormant in our being. I was very fortunate enough to be told that I was my great-granddad. If I had been a materialist, I would have every reason to doubt this, but I feel in my heart that that is the case. I have returned and I am him, it makes sense to me for it to be this way. But I have a new and different life to live now; it's just the curiosity factor that drags me back for a peek, if it is possible, at the past. There is a natural curiosity I believe that is in all of us, why do we want to know? Because it is natural for us to want to know where we came from and to where we are going. But the answer to that is far greater than you could ever imagine.

This unprovable issue we have of me being the reincarnation of my great-grandfather has committed me to giving it much thought and the only thing I can add to all of this information is the fact of how distant he was to me and how the few times the family ever talked about him. In fact, we didn't talk about him, as you know I didn't even know his first name. I can count on one hand the times he was talked about and it was only when my mother was alive, way back in the early nineteen eighties, over twenty years ago, as she died in 1984. The last time he was mentioned was at her brother's, my uncle's, funeral, but only in the light of him being a bit of a mystery to us all, of him operating on himself, that act causing him to die, and the fact that all the history of what happened then, had now been lost due to my uncle's death in April, 1996, He had remained silent throughout the rest of his life about his gruesome discovery, not mentioning the incident ever again (see appendix), so when I state that my great-grandfather was the farthest person from my thoughts when I received the information on me being him, he really was the farthest person from my thoughts. I can also state that in my estimation, had the incident of the near death experience not have happened to me, he would probably never have been thought of by me or any of the family again. Do you think of your great-grandfather very often? Maybe you think of your grandfather, but not your great-grandfather.

In most of the cases of known reincarnations, the subject has had some sort of recognisable link to their previous life. The obvious trap one must not fall into is to try to carry on with that past life, from where you left off, if you are able ever to remember it. The most important thing for anyone to do is to live this next life as your subconscious planned it in the spirit world in the first place, before you returned here to the earth.

I find myself at a disadvantage in tracing anything at all of my past life. This is because when I was a child, I was often taken to the Forest of Dean, Hazel Hill Drybrook, to stay with my grandparents. This was at least twice a year, right from when I was a baby. Later on it was in my school days; it was mostly in the school half terms and summer holidays, when Mum and Dad were at work. So, that being that case, everything I saw there in the area was familiar to me right from the very start. The chance to recognise any local place or location would be impossible, because everything would be so familiar to me anyway. It would be of no use or help in tracing my past life because who is looking for anything anyway and, really speaking, why should you be looking? The task is impossible. Confirmation, in most cases, cannot be gained. This must happen in the cases of almost all local rebirths, where the surroundings would be the same as when the person died and left this world, although it would depend on how long an absence it had been. Only those who are born to a different, unfamiliar area and then return to the place of a previous lifetime have any chance of recognising the familiar surroundings they once frequented. Then, they would have to have a suspicion, of a sort, to want to enquire.

After, say, fifty years the changes could be quite dramatic if there have been new buildings put up, new estates built, and the demolition of buildings taking place. The location alters dramatically, but I think almost everybody has had the feeling sometime of *dejavu*, when visiting some place or another that they think is familiar to them and think "I have been here before," but they just can't figure it out and think no more about it.

You must also take into account the power of your memory. Can you remember being born? Can you remember much of your childhood? Most of it, I bet, is only of the good bits and much more of the bad stuff, which is usually the best people can do. So to try and go back to a time before you were born is nigh on impossible. If I asked you to remember what you were doing a month last Thursday, you would struggle to answer unless there was something you always did on that day of the week, or unless it was something dramatic or traumatic or even very pleasurable that had happened to you. Otherwise your memory would be hard pressed to recall anything. This is because the automatic pilot has a junk filter, so anything trivial or habitual that happens is finally filtered out, as it is of no use to your mind. It works just like your e-mail junk filter that deletes all the junk messages after a certain time limit.

Some people get so curious they go to a hypnotist to be regressed to their past life. This can be done under hypnosis if so desired, but is not recommended by me and should only be done if it is of some benefit to the person, who should have a valid reason for doing it, not just for curiosity sake. Your past life is best left behind; it feels like a kind of cheating, anyway. In most cases you should be too busy living this life; we have enough to worry about. Why would you want to have to worry about what went on before; something that can't possibly be changed whatever you do, what's done is done? The only possible advantage to you is to know what wrongs you have done. You are then able to know how you can put them right. But that is where you cheat. You shouldn't know, that is why our memory is taken before our birth. We have to reset our tests. It is for each of us to work it out. In my particular case, I haven't been directly told of my mistakes, just that I have made some. I didn't do or finish the things that I should have; I have to work it out the same as everybody else and hope I get it right this time. Here though, I must confess that being told who I was has been a huge help to me, although I believe it's slightly different from me delving back into my past life. I feel it just about clears me of cheating.

Because of what the funeral report told me, I have a pretty good idea of what I did wrong. I will give the details of what I think it was and hope it doesn't upset too many people, because it's very critical of some religious beliefs. Here is how I think it goes then. The funeral report stated that my great-granddad attended the Congregational Church regularly and for some forty years, he was a member of the Congregational Men's Bible Class. To my way of thinking in these modern days, he was what I would call a bit of a bible puncher— I was a bible puncher, so it seems, in my last life! But there again I may be wrong, so I presumed this and looked up the Congregational Church on the Internet and found plenty. Most of the information I acquired referred to evangelical tendencies, which is preaching the gospel and looking for and trying to get converts. This represents, in my mind, a total misconception as to what we should do as evolving souls in the progression towards spiritual enlightenment. It is totally wrong to try and change or convert a person into a religion not of his or her choosing and one can inflict a serious delay in the progress of that person by trying to change their beliefs. The individual has to find his own way when he is ready and only when he is ready. The initial teaching he has absorbed in school and at church, when in his childhood, is either slowly understood or disregarded piece by piece; disregarded if it is found to be suspect to his logical way of thinking, but absorbed into his make up if it fits into it. This is when the individual will enquire about all the reasons of being. And if he, or she, asks for help and advice, it's then and only then that you should reveal what you think or know. It is better for the individual to search for and read about such things for himself by selecting appropriate literature. Hopefully this book will help and by writing it I make available a choice for an alternative outlook. It is a choice, yes or no, and maybe without forcing an opinion the reader can make up his own mind. If I was guilty of this unrecognised crime of forcing my beliefs onto others in my past life, I sincerely apologise and ask for forgiveness. I hope this statement about this unrecognised crime, because it is a crime, a crime against the soul, goes towards repairing the damage I may have caused. I am still working on any other failed task of mine and hope I can solve them during this lifetime. You just have to be so mindful all the time.

Be very wary of becoming a preacher, as you may well be preaching an untruth. In most cases, the only reason why any religion or cult would want converts is for their own gain. It is usually for money or to strengthen their egos to give them power over others. It is indeed a sad fact that the church thinks everyone is a sinner and never gives man the credit of ever finding his own way. You can be religious without belonging to any religion. Religion is within the individual; it is a private matter and should be left for those who wish to discuss the issues in open debate.

My great-granddad was found in the Meend enclosure at the Stenders, according to the inquest report. Only the old local residents of the area would know where that is, or was. Is it pronounced "me end?" Or "meand," but spelled "Meend?" I certainly don't know, but I do know that on one particular day during my childhood, while we were going for a walk, my family and I were walking up the Stenders, heading for the beech-walks at the top of the hill. This is the road leading out of Drybrook, which takes you on to Mitcheldean. On the right hand side of the road to us there was an enclosure. We saw it every time we came on the bus to visit our grandparents and then it was on the left hand side to us, viewing from the bus. It was a triangular, or wedge shaped, pen with fencing all the way round it. It was full of ferns, patches of high bracken, and gorse bushes. It had well trodden paths going through them made by the wildlife; it also had areas of coarse grass. It would have been about two acres in size and was unusual because most everywhere you go in the Forest of Dean is unfenced, common or forestry land. Because it was the first time we had had a chance to explore this area, my brother and I ran across the road to investigate, as boys do, but were immediately called back by our mother who told us never to go near there again. She never ever gave us an explanation as to why, she just said "I don't want you to go anywhere near there again" and we didn't. I may be wrong, but I think it is possible that that pen was the Meend enclosure, where my great-granddad had died. That, though, only the locals would know. I haven't been back there for over thirty years.

Chapter 4

Now that I have opened a can of worms, so to speak, in regard to reincarnation, I think it only right to thoroughly explain the indications and meanings of it all and tell you how I see it. I hope it clears up any misunderstandings and anomalies that have arisen.

But first of all we must regard and compare the time difference between our two busy dimensions, that of life here on Earth in the physical world (the third dimension), to life beyond death in the spirit world on the astral plane (the fourth dimension). This is given as one Earth year equals three cosmic minutes, so a cosmic minute in the spirit world equals four months on Earth. This will answer the question as to how I came to have so much information from my near death experience in only a few seconds. The time difference between the two dimensions though, doesn't seem to change or alter in any way to our consciousness. Everything seems to be going on at the same pace, regardless of which plane you are on, physical or spiritual. We can do so many more things in the time we have on the other side of life, the real side of life, because we are vibrating so very much faster there. So, a second of Earth time spent in the spirit world, is equivalent to two whole days here on Earth. I don't think this information is widely known because it is so fantastic and unacceptable to most materialists. Plus it turns the time I spent in the spirit world after my past life and the misfortune in the woods in the Forest of

Dean where I died to the time of my birth into this present life, from November 16th 1935, until June 23rd 1943, from seven years and seven months of Earth time, into just twenty-three minutes in spirit time. It makes you think; imagine if you live to be eighty years of age here on Earth. You will have left the spirit world for only four hours of spirit time. It is said that life on Earth is but a twinkling of an eye, now you know why, but I will go into more detail on the time difference in the next chapter.

A sad notation here with regard to people who have gone into a coma for one reason or another, they are what is known as astral travelling. They are exploring the spirit dimensions and are oblivious of the time difference. They have every intention of returning and know they must come back, but are completely engrossed in their activities there. They are not to know that their loved ones are waiting for them to return to their physical body and back to consciousness. There is no consolation for these loved ones here on Earth. With this time difference, they can only hope their loved one will return sooner rather than later. The person in a coma is not aware he has been away and is quite happy living his real life in the spirit world, with the ratio of one hour being equivalent to twenty years. As I said before, there is no indication of the time difference to alert their senses so they could possibly measure between the two dimensions. Also, time is of no importance in the spirit world because you have plenty of it. So, time is not a consideration. At best, you may try to call them back to their body by sending to them very strongly concentrated thoughts of where they belong. Picture all their favourite haunts, friends, and family and then think of them and you may get through whatever they are concentrating on in the world where they are. Don't give up; it is worthwhile to keep trying. You may just break through their concentration and help them return to their body.

Here we can include a fact of life. I have just read in the newspaper, after hearing it on the television news the previous day that on June 3rd, 2007, a Polish man woke up after being in a coma for nineteen years. It reached the world news and I thought it appropriate to include it here:

A Polish railway worker has woken after nineteen years of a coma to discover that his world has changed beyond all recognition. "When I went into a coma there was only tea and vinegar in the shops," Jan Grzebski, now 65, told a Polish news channel. "Meat was rationed and there were huge petrol queues everywhere."

Mr. Grzebski lost consciousness in 1988, after he was hit by a train. Doctors gave him only two years to live. But because of the tireless care of his wife Gertruda, who moved him every hour to prevent bedsores, he remained in good health. He was however, completely removed from the dramatic changes across the world. After regaining consciousness, he told his family that he had vague memories of the family gatherings and of his relatives talking to him, trying to provoke a response. There was plenty for them to tell him about, if they had wished to startle him with amazing news. When Mr. Grzebski lost consciousness in 1988, Lech Walesa, recipient of the Nobel Peace Prize in 1983, was back at work after years of house arrest. Within two years, communism had collapsed and M. Walesa was elected President of Poland with 75% of the vote. When he ran again in 2000, Mr. Grzebski's relatives would have pointed out, that only 1% of the electorate voted for him this time. By then, Poland had a market economy and communism was receding rapidly into the past, but the injured railwayman was still dead to the world. His wife, who was said by Mr. Grzebski's doctor to have "done the job of an entire intensive care team," continued to change his position every hour.

"I cried a lot, and prayed a lot," she said of those long and lonely years. "Those who came to see us kept asking, 'When is he going to die? But he's not dead.'

Gertruda Grzebski took no precautions to save her husband from shock when he came round and the miracle of modern Poland flooded his senses. He could not help noticing that people were complaining just as much as during the years of empty shops and martial law.

"Now I see people on the streets with cell phones and there are so many goods in the shops it makes my head spin," he con-

fessed. "What amazes' me is all these people who walk around with their mobile phones and yet they never stop moaning,"

Mr. Grzebski is still recovering the use of his body and is still being moved around in a wheelchair, but all seems set for a full recovery.

I comment here that when seeing him on the television news, I would say he had aged those nineteen years and did look sixty-five, if not a little older.

Sadly, there is no one to ask him the important questions that we all want to know and that is: do you, or can you, remember where you have been all this time? By the time these questions are asked he will surely have forgotten, especially with all the mesmerising new things that are all around him now. One thing could be gleaned from this rare incident by the medical profession is that Mr. Grzebski said he vaguely remembers the family gatherings. This means he was the closest to regaining his consciousness when he was being moved around in a lot of activity and was consequently being thought about by all his family; the ones that he is closest to. This joint thinking by his family seems to have interrupted his concentration in whatever he was doing in his coma and nearly brought him back each time there was a family celebration.

To return to our theme, the other problem a coma sufferer will encounter, as I did in my experience, is you do not remember a thing about what you have been doing or seeing. Everything happens so fast in the spirit world and the longer your activities there remain unknown to your consciousness, the less chance you have of recalling it. So unless there is a catalyst of some kind, it will remain in the subconscious untold. You will recall that it took three days and an M.R.I. scan to trigger my memory into action, combined with rest and relaxation. This period of time also allowed my brain to download and absorb the mass of information. So it seems we need a shock to the system, then relaxation, for a recall. We need to meditate then, so if ever anyone has a near death experience, you might have had quite an experience and it could be recalled if you take time out, relax, and try and remember. You never know what you might unfold. Enough for now, I will return to this later. I must press on with the reincarnation quest.

The first thing I suggest anyone who is interested does in this new outlook on reincarnation is to investigate from their own position within their family. I will do it methodically as we go on in this chapter, from the first born. We will start as if you were the first born child, go through the permutations of the family, and see where we finish. If it gets too bad or boring, skip the next few paragraphs because it can get very involved and complicated. I have a feeling I am going to regret this, but here goes.

Presuming you are a boy and the first child born to your mother, you will have descended from your father's group. This is the first circumstance to be discussed in many more situations that are possible in this situation; we will progress and deal with those as we go so don't jump to conclusions before we have completed the set. If your father's group family had a member ready to return, then it is more than likely you are that member.

It is possible you have been spasmodically watching your father from the other side (astral) of life, rather than your mother, in their lives down here on Earth. You have been waiting for the opportunity to come back to try once more, to learn your lessons, but mainly to stay within your cherished folks. You will have come back without any idea of how long you have been in your spiritual realm, unless you have been very privileged, or you planned it that way. In either case, it's very unlikely. I would say more or less impossible. I make this remark because we have only just found out about this situation; it has never been divulged before now, so it's pretty new to our understanding.

The next thing we have to do is check to see if your father was the eldest son or whether he has any brothers or sisters. If he was the eldest son, then it is a pretty good guess that you are from this group, your grandfather's group. It's the highest probability you can get and there is no situation closer to that. I don't think we need to expand any more on this first option, as it is perfectly straightforward.

If your father was the second child in his family, the younger brother, you would be coming from your grandmother's family group, your granddad's wife's family. This is on the same scale as the first option. So, you would investigate your grandmother's maiden name, as it is this group you have, in all probabilities, come from. We are still referring to the fact that you are the first born child and I further stipulate that in both cases, it does not always work out this way. Nothing is set in concrete. It might sound contradictory, but if there isn't anybody due to come back from the family group, the slot can be filled by the closest family group member, in order down a scale of priorities. In this second synopsis, it is very probable that the first choice is as stated and you come from your grandmother's group. It is just as straight-forward as the first analogy. This then explains the situation for the second born child, that whether a boy or a girl, they are most probably from the mother's group.

This brings us on to the first born son, coming from a third born son, i.e. your father being the youngest brother of three. Unfortunately, it is impossible to tell from which family group he comes from because as soon as you go from the first and second born, it becomes a lottery on who comes back and from where. But here goes as to where he is probably from. The options are: first from his grandfather's group, second from his grandmother's group, third and forth from his two sets of great-grandparents groups, and so on. Then again, he might even be starting a family group of his own.

There is no point in continuing any further down this road, it only leads to total confusion. What I suggest is that you just follow the pattern set out from the start. It acts as a sort of guide for the individual to follow and the further one goes back into the past, the more complicated it becomes, but you will see how we are all closely tied to one another. This is when you need your family tree records, starting with the dates of when your family members were born and the dates of when they died. Then you can see if there are any similarities or comparisons in the dates, the amount of time between each death and birth, and whether they tie in with anything or anyone in the family. There is a chance that a death date corresponds with a birth date, even in the same month; the birth date being, of course, after the death date and so on.

Now I will try to explain the daughter's part in all of this, starting with the first born being a girl. The same procedure is adapted as for the first born son, but the system alters when she has children because her first born child will come from her husband's family group. Her second born child will come from her father's family group, her third child will again revert back to the husband's group, but a further consideration has to come from her mother's family group. The female side of things always seem to complicate matters, but this is a very valid point. Under the normal run of things when we reach the third child, all the returning souls have taken up their place within the family, as the normal return is one for each partner. If there is another member of the husband's family to return, say from his mother's family which would be the obvious case, that soul takes precedence in the proper line of things. The soul wanting to return from the mother's side has to wait for the fourth child, if there is one, and there you have it. May I stress that the normal thing to happen is that the family needs are usually catered for.

Now I really don't want to go into this, but the second born daughter will come from her mother's family group. Her first born, again, will come from her husband's father's group, her second born child will come from either her father's or mother's family group, and her third from her husband's father's or mother's group or any family member from either side who is ready to return. We now have a tangle of families within a generation and to go on and try to explain a third daughter would be folly, because we start to get deeply involved. I think it wise that we call it a day. Remember, there is no guarantee that you are a family member, just the probability.

As a guide and from my personal point of view, I can relate to my father's situation again to clarify the situation. My father was a guest spirit to the Weaver surname family group; he was the sixth child and would probably have come from his mother's family group if he had not been a guest spirit. The complications that arose in the claim for his first born was further complicated by this situation, but as you know the claim was a successful one. Although he was a guest, he was still beholden to the Weaver family and was the only link left to that Earth name. As things have turned out, though, it shows it did not do them any good. It seems the Weaver family was destined to disband; they could not change their fate. The full details as to how the Weaver family got into this situation is as follows.

My granddad Weaver had eight children, four boys and four girls. His first born was a boy who managed to produce one son. This was my grandfather's first grandchild, all well and good for the continuation line, but this grandson never had children, so that link came to an end. His second born child was a girl who never had children, so this was an end. His third born child was a boy again, very handy to carry on the group line, but unfortunately he only had one child and that was a girl, a granddaughter who never had children. Again, it is the end of the line. His fourth child was a girl who never had children and his fifth child was a boy who never had children. His sixth born child was my father, who you know about; the seventh born child was a girl and the only one in the family who did not get married, she never had children. The eighth born child was a girl who married a first cousin. This was frowned upon and vigorously contested at the time, and caused a deep rift in the family. It was looked down on by most all the members of the family and she was disowned by the majority of them. Unfortunately, I never met her or knew I had another aunt until I was over twenty. I only met her once and that was at her husband's funeral. I did not see her again, as she died not long after. She had two sons who are both back in spirit and they never had children, so that was the end there, too.

My brother and I are the only surviving offspring of this big family, all of the rest are back in the spirit world. My situation as a Weaver is more or less finished in regard to family name and spirit lineage, because I am the second son and therefore come from my mother's side. I have three wonderful daughters and they have given me five wonderful grandchildren. My older brother is the only member of the Weaver family to continue the name; his first born child was a girl, a daughter who has no children. His second born child was a son who, in turn, has had a son, but there is a problem here with the linage. My brother's grandson will have come from his wife's family group because my brother's son was the second born child. He will still carry the Weaver name on, if this grandson chooses to have children, but it will only be from a third grandchild that a genuine Weaver can come back to this group unless other circumstances prevail. Otherwise, the Weaver family group will be reincarnating within another group of souls and it would probably be for the better if they did, so that they can further their progress on a different course.

This bit of history I hope will explain how it works. One thing I would like to say here is about my father. My father was a devoted gentleman and a law abiding citizen; I know he loved us very much. He worked long hours to provide for us, his immediate family, and he kept us in food and clothes. He never raised a hand to either me or my brother and put his duty to us foremost in what he did. The Weaver family dogma of not believing there is anything after death was his big dilemma, although a few family members went through the motions of having a bible. That was the limit of their commitment, so I hope my mother managed to get through to him before she died. I questioned him about it on occasions and suggested he give it another thought, but his words always echoed in my mind. They were, "Why do they have torture chambers in Gloucester Cathedral? They forced people to pray and they do this in the name of their god, no, once you are dead you are dead."(This statement of there being torture chambers in the cathedral may have been a reference to the dungeons there; I personally have never been there to check it out.) He would always say that, just like a record.

"That's beside the point," I would say to him in answer and say that the church has nothing to do with believing in life after you die. The fact is, they don't prescribe to it in any realistic way.

I don't believe he ever gave it a thought; he was never a deep thinking man. It was as if he had been programmed for just one thing and that was to provide for his family. All I know is you could not get a better, ordinary man who did his duty. I am sure he has been well rewarded. And if you do this throughout your life, I'm sure you won't regret it either, at least you will not have harmed yourself. I know my father didn't seem to have any afflictions, maybe a little bit of spite for his cousin, but he was my father and as children we never questioned what our parents did.

He may not have gained enlightenment, but he has given himself a good starting point for his next attempt, with very few burdens of past bad deeds or debts. The only thing I think he will regret is being influenced by the other members of his family in regards to not staying in touch with his youngest sister, a very sad state of affairs indeed. It affected my brother and me by not being able to know our aunt, uncle, or our two cousins. They would have been older cousins to us, but I am sure we would have enjoyed being in their company. I know my father had an acute disliking for his cousin; maybe this was his plight, to accept the marriage of his youngest sister to his cousin. It makes you wonder, we all must remember that we are all equal. It doesn't pay to think we are any different.

With this tragic, but silly and childish situation, I will take this opportunity to explain what damage a situation like this can really do. This damage is caused by any individuals demanding their influence and opinions be obeyed by another person, usually a relation or partner, in other words, somebody believing they own a person because they are a parent, older brother or sister, or partner. It is usually within the family and it has devastating effects and consequences. Beware of power possessed people too; they are the curse of the earth. We as individuals have a free will and at the end of our lives we, and only we, take the full consequences of all that we have done. Nobody else takes any blame or responsibility for the decisions and actions we have made or taken during our life. So it is only right for us to rebel when any unreasonable demand is made upon us.

Earlier in this book I explained how we tend to see only our own points of view and it is very difficult to change our minds from the ways in which we were brought up and trained in our younger days. In this situation we have to cleanse selfishness from our system; otherwise we entrap ourselves to yet another round of existence here on earth.

By all accounts, my uncle (dad's cousin and how he described him) was a womanizer; he apparently had an eye for my father's two youngest sisters. He eventually married the youngest, but I think we must be a little reasonable here. We all know that in the early stages of our lives, in our late teens and into our early twenties, the attraction to the opposite sex is foremost in our minds, especially a virile young man's. I can imagine my father being quite protective of his two younger sisters and would have defended their honour to the last breath. But when you examine this scenario from both sides you can build up a better picture and have a more balanced view of things. And when you take into consideration that my uncle and aunt stayed together for the rest of their lives, there must have been a special bond between the two of them, a special relationship. This is a typical relationship described in a previous chapter. Anything is possible when you are in love and these two people were certainly close to that. Who knows? They could well have been two spirits, reincarnating just to be back together again in the physical world and that was the only way they could do it. This is quite a valid point; they would have to endure all the frustrations of family ridicule, prejudices, and persecutions, which they would expect to get and certainly did get. They thought it was a price worth paying, just to be with one another again. But look at the turmoil and havoc it caused within the Weaver family. Every member of the family was affected, each in a different way depending on what view each member placed on the situation, but that is another story. You can quite imagine what effect it would have on your family, or anybody else's family, just by thinking about it.

This obsession, by the way, that we have of inbreeding within the family creates another problem. Besides it being against the law, we are taught that it is wrong and that it will lead to mutations and the like. But that is incorrect; scientists and researchers have found there are no deformities or any other mutations caused by inter-family breeding. The one thing against this practice is to the immune system of that family. It never gets a boost from another source to strengthen it against any new diseases. If some nasty virus were to strike, all members of that family could very well be wiped out. This has happened in the Amazon rain forest with the outbreak of smallpox amongst the isolated native Indians brought by the European explorers.

If you refer to the story of Lot's family in the bible, this is an example of where all offspring were normal. The Egyptians were always practicing inter-breeding and we think we know why.

There is the story of the Mesopotamian gods; they set us a real bad example as they were forever inter-breeding with their own family. If the gods never thought it a crime, why are we taught that it is? I must admit that the law has been relaxed for some time now. It is accepted that cousins can marry and is now quite common place. If it were the only way left in preserving a human vehicle for us souls to have a physical body and to be able to progress in the material world, then it would have to be. After all, we are only creating a vehicle so we can continue to have a temple to house our spirits in and to work on the physical plane. Without the temple body we are stranded. Let's hope we never reach that position.

Chapter 5

At the beginning of the previous chapter, I dropped a bomb shell by stating the time difference between the two dimensions, that of the astral plane and that of the physical plane. Although this is only one aspect of the many time differences applied to each dimension that are there, the higher the dimension the faster the speed of vibration. We are only concerned with the two, so to try and make it more understandable, let's have some examples. These examples will be better understood if we say they are relative only to the persons involved. Time is not the same to everybody, we can say time has a relative meaning to everybody, but it seems different on occasions. This is according to what people are doing at that instant, so it is relative only to the person or persons involved. To try and explain this, we set up an imaginary exercise as follows.

You put four chairs in the centre of a square room so that each chair was facing a different wall, say north, east, south, and west, and then you sat a different person on each chair and instructed them to look at the wall for the time duration of one hour. Then you put a sound and light omitting barrier is placed between each person so they cannot tell what is happening in the other chairs. This would make each of them totally isolated.

Moving in a clockwise direction, on the north wall for the first person, we have placed a large clock with the usual hour, minute, and second hands. This person has to watch the time continuously until the hour is over. He must not do anything else other than just watch the clock.

On the next wall, the east wall, for the second person we have a movie screen showing subjects he is interested in.

Next, on the south wall, for the third person we have a computer game representing a treasure hunt, with a time limit of, again, one hour, where winner takes all. You have sixty clues and you have to solve a clue a minute. There are death traps throughout the game and you are given six lives. If you lose all your lives you are able to start again, as long as it is within the hour. The prize is won only on completion of the task. Unbeknownst to the player, the game has no ending; it can never be finished; that sounds a bit like our lives.

Finally, we come to the last chair facing the west wall. For the fourth person, we make the wall pitch black. He has no light or sound available to him. He is totally isolated, even more so than the others. Now for the purpose of this exercise, let us say that we are able to induce him into a coma the instant the hour starts. This is not generally possible, but it will help in the understanding of this exercise. This person is then free to travel the astral world above the physical plane, but will be instantly brought back at the end of the hour. Lastly, you must imagine you are these four people, you are experiencing everything they are experiencing, and you have to do this for the exercise to work. When the hour has finished, the four experiences can be analysed.

Now the outcome is that you can do the first three tasks easily. Maybe the first one is not that easy, but the first task will feel that it has taken the longest. It will seem in fact, that it has taken ages; your mind will have wandered many times because it was so bored. In this situation time drags by very slowly. The second task will feel about right, an hour will have passed and it will feel just like an hour has gone by. This is the norm when you are occupied. The third task will seem to be over very quickly, in fact too quickly, because it is one of those times when we are in a situation where we never have enough time to do the things we want to do. You always run out of time. So the three time experiences so far can be described as being different in duration, but relatively speaking they took exactly the same amount of time. It is interesting to note here that the speed of action in the three tasks is relative to the condition, i.e. slow in the first task, normal in the second, and fast in the third. But with the forth and last task, we will find it a little different from the normal run of things. Let us see what the last task produces. Although the time duration was exactly the same, the last person spent the hour in a coma. I can tell you roughly what he said the instant he was aroused and that is, "well, when is this exercise going to start?"

The person in a coma would have no comprehension of any time passing. He will have lost the hour completely. He was somewhere else, his physical body was still working and ageing here on earth, but his conscious mind was with his spirit, exploring this freedom in the spirit world that his mind is naturally familiar with. He would have been fully engrossed in what he was doing wherever he had gone, so when he was rushed back to his body, and because he did so much in the other dimension, his mindless physical brain could not absorb anything he had seen or done during that earthly hour. There is just a complete blank, even of time, so the brain tells you that nothing happened. That's because the brain doesn't have the capacity or scope to cope with that sort of influx of information in the time allowed (instantaneously). There is a safety mechanism called the mentality that stops the brain from overload. As you now know the brain is only a computer and if you think about this, one hour in spirit represents twenty years in earth time! To cram twenty years of events into an instant transfer is impossible. It is also incomprehensible to us that such a time difference can exist. Your mentality is you're built in safety valve; whatever you have trained your mentality to accept is your limit of comprehension. It will tell you how much you are prepared to accept into your being, so it's what type of mentality you've got that governs your outlook. This at times can be our biggest drawback and may limit our progress; this is not to say that you have to accept everything you come across as real. It takes the power of discrimination to do that, but be brave and just keep an open mind. Anything is possible, but keep it all within your comprehension or you could end up in a mental home.

To again help in understanding this better, we know that it takes time to download material onto a computer, therefore we can say in comparison there is no difference and it is exactly the same for our brains. Our five physical senses send signals to our brain and in turn the brain sends signals to our mind, where they are recorded and stored in the subconscious memory bank. That's, of course, if these signals are of any use. Most of the material we absorb today is just trivia and is of no use to us at all.

We have access to this memory bank through the brain, but we have difficulty when we come across material that our brain, during this lifetime, hasn't put in there. This is going on mostly during our sleep. We generally only recall things that we have had happen to us in our present physical life of awakened state. But I have had this experience of seeing some of this other material and to explain it. I can only liken it to viewing some of your old photographs of different events you have taken during your lifetime. You then come across a picture you cannot remember ever taking, but it seems so familiar to you and is not out of place. Try as you may, you cannot recall ever taking it, so you accept it and move to the next one. But then, when you look for it again, the picture is gone and you then can't find it. This is how it seems to me; I get it when I am daydreaming sometimes and I try to recognise what it is that I am seeing, like recalling a dream. I try my hardest to make some sense of the quick flashes of these familiar pictures I am seeing, but to no avail. Because they are so quick in passing through my conscious mind, I cannot quite make out what they are. Therefore, I cannot understand them because I haven't got the full picture. This is most annoying and I put it down to an incomplete or faulty download by my brain. Having been on a journey in the spirit world when asleep then, on returning and because of the different rates of vibrations, only fragments of the journey have managed to get through. Let's give this another analogy by comparing it with when you try to get information from your computer without the correct software. You get this oblong box notice with a blue band across the top, with a multi-cord ring tone that goes drrrrunggg, accompanied with a big red "ex" in a circle, telling you that the function requested cannot be read or activated without its driver; or the program is not recognised, please insert a disc; or the required software is unavailable please refer to the program and install the correct driver. So it seems our brains respond in the same way as a modern computer to material it doesn't recognise.

This brings us to the word, "recognise," an underestimated word with a powerful meaning. If we say we recognise something, it means it was known to us before. We cognised it or understood whatever it was and whatever we saw. This happens when we read or see something, even when it is new to us and seeing it for the first time in this particular lifetime, we are recognising it again. In other words, we knew it in the first place.

It is the mind part of us that is always awake and goes off somewhere to live when we are asleep or knocked unconscious. The body that we live in, including the poor old brain, is left behind with no attendant other than the autopilot and therefore is left out of things in the real sense of life. We are left out, no, we are locked out of our spiritual life, but this is really for our own good. So when the mind comes back to the body, it has no reason at all to transfer any of the wealth of information it has experienced back down to the body here on earth. It has no need to. Some of the times when your mind is trying to telling you something, that you should know, is when you are conscious and in a daydream, this is a time when you are at-one with yourself, (treasure the moment), and should take note if possible of the aspects you are daydreaming about. Isn't it funny how we always say when asked about what we were thinking, we usually answer "oh, nothing, nothing at all," because those thoughts are personal.

The earthly body is only used down here to gain physical experiences; it cannot be used on the higher, faster dimension. So why transfer incomprehensible knowledge back to your personal robot machine that you only use on the slower third dimension? There is a very good reason for this and that is because we haven't got the capacity in our physical brains to hold all this knowledge and, to add to that, it's not much use to us down here anyway. Do you tell your house where you have been when you get home? You certainly don't tell it where you are going when you go out; this is basically on the same principal as to how the mind, our minds, think and work. The body is just a vehicle like your car is to you.

The mind works mainly from the spiritual dimension, our normal home. It is the dimension that we are all used to when we are in spirit and without the hindrance of the physical body. Our minds are so used to it that we don't even sense it is there when we are down here on earth. Every time our minds go there, life is so familiar; it is accepted as the normal to us because that is where our life really is. We get glimpses of it now and again in unusual circumstances, like coming back from a dream after being startled into awakening and then remembering fragments of it, or when being involved in an accident that, at the time, you thought your life would end, but that's how it works. I hope I have explained the never ending life existence we have in the spirit world clearly for you. It is difficult for any individual to grasp any new information on this subject, especially in regards to a speed time zone and one that cannot be proved. You will just have to wait and see. We, the finite, cannot know and describe the infinite because the infinite is like a dream to us.

How do you explain it to a person who has just missed death by a whisker, who says to you that they have just seen the whole of their life flash before them, just before they nearly met their fate? The logical and material way of thinking would be to say, how could that possibly happen? There is no time for it to be possible. If you were to tell that person that the rush of adrenalin the near miss from death caused, actually threw your consciousness into the next dimension for a split second or two and this allowed you to see all the major events in your life. They would think you were crazy. Would you say to them that it is quite feasible for this to happen, you know! Well, the answer is "no," I don't think you do. They would look at you with at least a deep frown of suspicion on their face. But these are the most often spoken words of the individuals who have experienced such a near death incident: it is a well known fact.

You cannot really comprehend how long it takes to view your whole lifetime either. For argument sake, let's say you have just seen the whole of your life flash before you. Some parts of it go past very quickly and some parts of it move slowly. When you are eventually in this situation after you've passed over from this life and you are viewing all of your life, you will have to feel the emotions that go with each experience you had. Then to add to that, you have to feel the emotions and effects your actions had on all the other people you loved or hated. Their emotions and feelings have to be experienced by you, too, to complete the cycle, so it would take a little while. But in this brief glimpse of your life, the mental part of your brain stops all the trimmings from coming through because it can't cope. You just get the pictures and you've probably seen twenty odd years worth of major events in your life go by in a split second.

It is important to mention here, to save any unnecessary confusion on the subject, that when a person manages to astral travel consciously or normally unconsciously (that's leaving ones physical body and travelling as a ghost), the time factor remains the same while the soul is on the physical earth plane and lower astral. It only changes when the soul moves up to the spirit world so the individual's mind can travel on either of the dimensions at his desire. To know what causes the mixed up dreams we get when we awake in the morning is when the two places are visited during the one sleep period and where the mentality has allowed some information to sift through to the brain. It is usually the normal time zone material we are able to recognise that mainly gets through. The confused brain changes anything out of the ordinary into something familiar to make some sort of sense out of the jumble it has received at such a fast rate, hence the reference to the weird dream. If I explain in detail what happened to me during my near death experience here, it will give you another picture regarding the time difference I described in chapter four and in this chapter, and how your brain makes things acceptable. I am going to explain as thoroughly as I can, what my physical brain experienced and led me to accept and, what happened to me. What I went through while I remained conscious in my NDE.

The black goo started to swirl all around me at about the height of my knees, as I stood facing the water closet. A feeling of nauseating giddiness came over me. The swirling black goo had flecks of grey, silvery, streaks in it, forming a pattern not unlike iron fillings tracing a magnetic field of a magnet. The feeling was most unpleasant to my physical body and added to the groin pain that I had. My thought was "this is it, I'm going to die" panic was setting in. This is because it was familiar to me in some way. Recognising that this was the death process setting in, (of the soul leaving the body), remembering it from the last time, and, help! I had too much to do before this could happen. The swirling mass was slowly engulfing me as I turned to go out of the closet and return into the bedroom. But before I rounded the door pillar it had completely engulfed me. My brain must have gone into survival mode at this time, as I could still consciously feel what was about me and I was concentrating so hard. It was most important that I stay conscious on the physical plane, as the possibility of me going over was imminent. This is the moment, when I called out to my wife to get an ambulance, saying I think I am dying. Holding onto the door pillar, I felt as though all the life had gone from me. Leaving me with no strength for my physical support, and giving me a feeling, my very bones had been whipped away from me. Expecting to collapse, I made a lunge towards my bed which was two meters away from the doorway. To my surprise I made it. I knew this, as I felt the soft duvet covers on my face and under the front of me. Not knowing for how long I lay there before I heard my wife ask me, if I really did want her to call an ambulance. She was stood by me at the side of the bed and the light was on.

After reflecting on this experience, I came to understand why Para-medics concentrate on keeping injured victims conscious and awake while waiting for medical help, or while in freezing cold conditions not to fall asleep. It is that border line between life and death, and the secret is to stay conscious.

Now we have to work out how long it took me to return to my bed, from inside the water closet, and how long it took my wife to respond to my call and get out of bed. Then walk around to my side of the bed, turn on the light by the door and then come to my side. I am sure that my spirit had left me before I was turning around to re-enter the bedroom. Because the swirling mass, had by then completely engulfed me and a change to my senses had occurred. I was now in auto pilot mode.

Retracing my footsteps from this time would amount to approximately five seconds, it could well be more but we stay on the side of caution. Now from the time I called to my wife and for her to realise what was happening and to get up and come to my side we have to estimate again on the side of caution. This time would amount to, no less than ten seconds, it could well be more, before she asked me about an ambulance and when I realised I had made it to the bed. And then to find the pain had subsided considerably. This is the point I believe, when my returning spirit was back in my body. At a conservative estimate, the time would be fifteen seconds, thirty days of earth time. Quite a reasonable time, for me to obtain the material that I had gathered, or was instructed with. But for my brain to gather up the information, and similar to a computer download would be. It was not available to me for three days.

In the morning, when I awoke my brain had recorded the physical side of my experience, put it neatly into a normal category and everything was as it should be for me to carry on as if no other incident had occurred. And that is what the brain does; I was unaware of anything else, except the heavy head. Which I now know was my brain downloading all the information that my mind was allowing to come through, while I carried on as normally as I could, oblivious of this action taking place. The outcome as you know is what you are now reading.

Did you know that if you have not succeeded in completing your tasks down here on earth after completing your life span, you are sent straight back to try again? Due to the time difference, this can sound confusing. Between being on the earth plane, where time seems to take ages, to when you are on the spiritual plane, where it becomes only a matter of hours, gives you plenty of time to sort things out.

When you are on the spiritual plane, you can prepare and plan another lifetime quite easily in a matter of what would be earth minutes. No doubt you will have a well earned rest while you are there, but even that should only take an hour or so. This would be incomprehensible to us down here on the earth if we didn't understand the time difference. To make it a little plainer, just to be sure you know it, let us do another little exercise. You have a reel of film that takes, let us say, a whole day to watch all the way through at the normal speed. Imagine being able to watch the whole film in just half a second and still see as much as you would watching it at the normal speed. So you would put it in the projector and wind it from one reel to another in half a second and see all the film, which would be the difference. It would be as if time had stood still, in other words, you were able to vibrate at a far greater rate. It would be like being in a situation where everyone but you was stationary; you could move things around and alter events as you wished. You would be moving so rapidly that nobody would be able to see you. Most likely this happens to us at times here on earth on the physical plane when we are in danger, but it's for you to decide on whether or not this happens. Although, when you think, some people have miraculous escapes from death; it's happening all the time. Doesn't this even make you wonder a little!

This leads me into the time span of our planned lives and our own fate. If you are quite sensitive, it will appear to you that on certain occasions you were saved certain mishaps. This type of thing is happening all the time, but we hardly notice it. I'm just saying that some of the time we are being looked after, especially if we are doing the right things, the things we are supposed to be doing. But that's not why it happens. It is to help in getting you to the end of your allotted life span, the time you planned to do down here, especially if you are doing well. Tragedies cannot always be avoided, or should I say tragedies sometimes can be avoided, but you have the responsibility of looking after yourself. If you are downright foolhardy, just beware and be prepared for the outcome.

Be aware of those signs that are around you, too, they are present all the time. Use your intuition to sense them; they are given names like omens, premonitions, gut-feelings, instincts, etc. You will do well to take notice of them; it is your subconscious (sixth sense) telling you something you should at least consider.

An instance of a personal experience I had, of one type of this phenomenon, is during my time as a sales rep for a tobacco company in the early 1970s, when I was selling cigarettes and tobacco to the retail shops. Every morning I awoke while doing this job, and I mean every morning, I was in a state of depression. This situation gradually worsened the longer I remained selling these products. I became so desperate and depressed that I had to get out of this field of employment for my own peace of mind. After only seven months in the job, I was able to change my employment and get out of that situation. It was not an easy thing to do, but straight away my life lifted out of that dark, depressing state and was so uplifting, you would be amazed.

It seems that when we go to sleep we are subjected to a battering from our over-soul for doing the wrong things in our lives and we get a right old rollicking from it during the hours of our sleep. I believe this is a major factor in causing the clinically depressed people who eventually commit suicide when ignoring or not understanding these warnings. This is the time when we are most in touch with our over-soul, who tries to keep us on course and to put us on the right path to follow in our lives down here. I was the unsuspecting instigator of supplying this death enhancing, deadly, habit forming smoking sticks (cigarettes). They were destroying people's lives and I was being informed, via my over-soul, that by doing so I was also harming myself. So I had to change my employment to fix it.

The more recent premonition I had was what I explained earlier in this book, about whether to tell my story or not. This is just an example of how it works, so take note. It seems to me that there is only a certain amount of tolerance the over-soul will put up with, especially if you are amassing bad debts of karma. An extreme case would be of a person out to kill others, such as a bomb maker and the like; they usually get blown up themselves in the end to stop their bad karma from overloading. How these sorts of people can live with themselves I will never know. They must have so much pent-up hate for their fellows, it just beggar's belief, but it takes all sorts to make a world. They certainly haven't any conscience; their egos have completely taken over and suppressed it.

If we return to our subject, there is no time limit in coming back from your death. The only obvious requirement is that you will have had to have died before you can be reborn; this allows you to occupy a baby born only hours after your death. This would represent the extreme limits, though, for a quick return; I would hope that you would get at least a little respite before you took another leap back into this hell school down here on earth.

These places, when they become available, are usually used up by the unfortunate souls who have committed suicide, having committed the worst possible crime to oneself, you then have to pay the price. The reasoning for this is that if you had the strength to kill yourself, you have proved that you had the strength to live.

There is no compromise in the case of a suicide. The poor soul only gets compassion from other souls who can only hope he doesn't repeat his act. He only gets advice; it is he who has to take the action not to do it again. If he does, his lives become more horrendous each time he takes his life and if he keeps doing it, when he gets to the bottom of his pit there is an even deeper one for him or those souls to fall into. It's a very long, hard haul back up. Nothing is worth committing suicide for, I repeat, nothing; it can never ever be justified.

We must also take into consideration the fact that they have cut their lives short from their planned full life span, the one they had created and planned before they came back. On this basis and because of the strict cosmic laws governing the act of suicide, the soul is sent straight back to finish this pre-booked time span of his life. Whatever the remaining time period amounts to, he returns for only that time span. So if the poor, misguided soul commits suicide when he is, say, twenty-five, with a planned life span of eighty years, he has to return to live the remaining fifty-five years that are left first, plus the time he was away in the spirit world re-covering, before he can continue with his evolution, where he gets the chance to choose and plan another life.

Although a lifetime on earth seems a long time, our lives down here are very short; but this does not seem to be the case to us while we are down here. Our consciousness is taken away from us when we have gone to sleep. Unlike the spirit and mind, the physical body, no matter to whom it belongs, has to be recharged by sleep after a day's activity. And while our bodies and brains are sleeping, our mind and spirit is away doing the busi-ness, living a totally different existence to what we know and un-derstand. This is how it is and the majority of the people will be happy with this arrangement. Life down here is complicated enough as it is, let alone for us to worry about the life to come after we die. All we know is that we have a life to come and it's best to leave it at that, because we can't even speculate on what that life might be.

It is just as well to be prepared for it though, because we wouldn't want to miss the opportunity to experience our transition from this life to that life consciously. It is in our interest to be in control where possible, so we must stop being tossed and thrown about by the normal flow of the stream of life and take the reins of our own destiny. We learn more quickly and better that way.

Chapter 6

The dying experience has been well documented over the ages; it is the only certain sure thing in our lives that we have to look forward to. This does not mean we want it now, the longer we can put it off the better, because our learning never stops. The general synopsis goes a bit like this.

First we look from the point of view of the people left behind after a loved one has died, meaning passed over. And accordingly, looking in a purely material and physical aspect, when you die you are dead. There can be no argument about that; it is a very true statement, when you're dead you are dead, but that is just the body. The general point of view we have of our relations or friends at their death is, that the people we loved and lived with were at one moment teeming with that sparkle of life and in the next, have become just a lump of dead meat. The shell and home to a spirited person has become just a lifeless hulk. After knowing the individual who once occupied this shell, how can you not believe that they have gone somewhere else?

You cannot escape from this reality if you are a deep thinking person and you know in your heart they have moved on, on along their journey to another existence. Their consciousness alone cannot just be stubbed out and be for nothing. It has to have a purpose, but we are never allowed to know what that is, all we know is that we will never see our loved one alive on the physical plane on the earth ever again. This brings us to the most heartbreaking emotions in our lives, which we have to endure and, in some cases, these are too much to bear. This grieving can last for a very long time and gives us all the more reason to get out of this repetitive sequence where we have trapped ourselves into this wheel of life that brings us more sorrow and pain than it does pleasure.

We accept with courtesy the statements of our religious authorities, even if it is their illusion, when some of them tell us that our loved ones will be resurrected, rise from the ground, and live again. I suppose it is hypothetical on their behalf, but it just cannot be possible. The body you once possessed cannot be brought back to life, besides, it would be in a right old rotten mess and in no fit state for you to be able to use it again.

This is obviously a misinterpretation of the religious teachings of our ancestors and it is not the first time for it to have happened. Just imagine the poor old pharaoh coming back and getting inside his old mummified corpse instead of reincarnating into a new body that grows into a fit, virile, handsome man. He certainly wouldn't attract any young females in his decrepit old shell. No doubt this is where the ideas of the mummy horror films came from and are based on this misunderstood doctrine. The ancient teachings, tell us that there is life after death, not in the used body we have left behind, but in a new one that is yet to come, yet to be reborn for your use, if you have to come back to the earth again. Or, to materialise into the new world that is awaiting us when we have completed our lessons down here.

So, we now come to the individual, who can be you or me, who is about to pass over from our present world into the life in the hereafter. It makes no difference if you are in good health or failing fast, the process and the outcome is the same. The only problem we have is that we are not prepared for it, not even if we have been given an accurate time for the event of our death to occur. This is because few people ever talk about the only certain thing we are guaranteed in life and that is to die.

We all worry and get quite concerned about it, but we never investigate what happens to us when we die. This is an absolutely crazy state of affairs, as we prepare to do nearly everything else in our lives, so why not prepare for our death? In the next few paragraphs I will pass on what I have managed to glean from the various religious doctrines that tell us what to expect when it happens to us. The most authentic are those from the countries of Tibet and India, but the general trend is the same in any country wherever you go that has recorded death experiences. Most of it, however, comes from the ancient writings of long ago. This knowledge is not supposed to upset your thinking, all you have to do is read it, store it only if it suits your needs, and then forget it until you may need it when you come to meet your fate.

If you are lucky enough to be in the position of slowly passing in old age, you have at least been expecting something to happen to you; it is when the unexpected happens to you that it can be a little different, although the result is the same. I will continue with the old age theme first and fit in, where appropriate, the other cases, but there is very little difference, the process is virtually the same. There is only one way of dying and that is when the spirit leaves the body for good. The body dies; although there are many different ways of being killed, but the result after is the same?

As you start to die, your body fades into a state of no energy. You are now entering the first stages of the transition into the coming real world. This is quite a pleasant feeling, one of "at last I can let go." Your age-old aching bones and inefficient body is at last letting go of its claim on you, it can no longer cling to your soul. You will be able to hear the sounds and voices of everybody who is around you as you gradually transfer out of your physical body. Be determined as possible to stay conscious, stay alert! You really need to be in control of your own destiny now. People who don't know this allow the automatic process to take over here and valuable knowledge is missed.

During this process of passing, hopefully there will be no hysterics or powerful loud mourning for you by any of the persons present. Otherwise, this can cause you to get upset and lose your concentration. It may cause you to become emotional and panic stricken. Be mindful of your plight and you will be okay; you will be okay anyway, but this is an opportunity for you to have a great experience. It is one you have been having many times before, but may not have realised this until it is all over. The majority of people in the western world do this, they just let the process take its own course and a long time after their death they become conscious and wonder where they are. Don't let this happen to you, remember, this is a very personal thing that is happening to you so take control, it is your death. Tell your loved ones, if you get the chance before you die, not to get too upset at your passing. You will be seeing them again soon, so please control your emotions and you will be able to leave in peace, tell them that.

You are now in the exit mode; closing down your computer brain and all your other organs, your body is shutting down and will no longer be able to be reactivated. You may feel a little tug, don't worry if you don't, it means you are having a smooth exit, but it is now the beginning of the separation of your soul from your body. You will slowly materialise above your old body, usually horizontal to it and floating above it. You will probably find that you are on the opposite end to how you were lying, your head being where your feet were. If you have managed to keep calm, are still conscious, and your soul has fully withdrawn, you have managed the first stages of leaving your old body. You will start to feel a gentle sway, as though you were floating in a small boat. You are now in what is called the lower astral plane. This is where the two planes meet and you are in the lowest frequency vibration of the astral world, which has myriads of different frequency levels for the accommodation of such a diverse scale of mixed up evolving souls.

Although you might not have noticed yet, you should feel exhilarated beyond your wildest dreams. Your attention will be on looking down on the scene below you, so take it all in. It is likely that you will have company by now from the spirit world. If you don't, do not despair or worry, they will come to you if you want them there with you. The choice is yours, you just think and they arrive, or you may wish to remain independent. I don't know how much time is allotted for you to linger here, but take your time; take in all that you can, it's your record, your passing, and your over-soul will move you when it is ready. It usually takes up to three days for all your essence to evacuate your physical body, so if your body is moved in the meantime, don't panic. You gather up together no matter where your body is taken.

You will feel a gentle tug around the time when you have to leave. In this next stage you will find that all your surroundings start to fade, like a television picture fades out, then you will experience a feeling of rising up. It is not up into the sky, just a feeling of rising as your vibrations are increasing. You will find yourself in what could be described as being in a long, dark tunnel with a very small light at the end of it. It will feel like you are being held back by thick, sticky, black treacle that slows your progress down, making it hard going.

Some people see a very long staircase, stretching way up into shining white clouds, which they have to climb up to get to where they should be. You can now see that it is going to take a little effort, but isn't that what we have to do in life to get to where we want to go? If you don't make an effort you don't get a thing of any value. You don't get to know, either, and knowledge is what we are here for.

In this sticky, swirling, black syrup, it's not syrup it just feels like syrup; you will have noticed this glimmer of light in the far distance, hence the description of a tunnel. This varies in brightness in accordance to the preparations you have made in your life down on earth and what you as a person believed to be real in that life. This is where your knowledge comes into play and now you have read this. If you didn't already know, you have to head for that light. Go to the light is what should be said to the ghosts who are trapped here on earth, so they can be released from their entrapment. Many souls, who do not understand what this is and don't know what to do, reject the light and head in the other direction. This is because the spirit world light, when it is first seen, is too bright for them and seems to be painful to their eyes. This lack of understanding can interrupt their progress a great deal. They become the lost souls who have not accepted a belief of a life after they die, or who have no spiritual inclination whatsoever. This black, sticky void can also be referred to as the place in which people have called hell. With all the blackness swirling around them and because of the sticky sensation, which seems to cling to them' they think they are being pulled down into the blackness of hell; this is purely their imagination working overtime. It is quite understandable when you consider these strange, unfamiliar surroundings these poor souls find themselves in, or any soul who has been caught up in this situation. They would refer to it as such. Many souls remain here on this low plane of vibration, close to the physical plane, but not belonging to it; not knowing where to go. And, until they realise the light is the only alternative direction, this is where they remain. Some find their way back to their old haunts where they were living on the earth, where they have a strong memory of something specifically important that happened to them during their lifetime, hence the existence of ghosts and the haunting phenomenon. In famous cases of any haunting the entities who are haunting no matter where it is, feed from the thoughts and mental energies released by the enquirers and visitors to the haunted site. With these visitors thinking of the departed person and also thinking they might see something, they become fearful. The ghost then feeds on their fear (mental energy) and this is the source of its energy.

The thick black void (sticky syrup) is the space between the two time zone dimensions and has to be crossed to get to your home. Swim, walk, jump, crawl, even relax completely and think your way there, but head for the light and only to the light. Thinking yourself there is the best way, but do something to urge your way forward, as long as you move to get to it. Whatever you do is usually hard work and not always plane sailing, but take it as it comes. Just get to the light do not get distracted; you are really being born again, into the astral world. Any distraction can delay or upset a smooth transition to the spirit world and, because that is your only goal, it should have your complete and utter attention. Remember the words of the twenty-third Psalm and the third verse. *"Yea though I walk through the valley of the shadow of death I will fear no ill, for thou art with me."* This has been written for the guidance of the soul in its passing from one world into the next.

The effort is worth it, the same as when you have to climb the huge staircase; it can seem to take ages, but you will get there in the end. As you enter the light or white clouds, if you came by the stairs, you are entering the new time zone and a part of the spirit world. The beauty is boundless. Now you will appreciate the effort you made to get here, the effort was raising your vibrations to the speed required for you to reach your destination, this glorious spirit world. You may wonder why it takes so much effort, more for some than others. It is because the part of your soul that has lingered so long in the physical dimension down here on the earth has gotten so used to vibrating so slowly that only a great effort on your behalf can increase it up to the required rate. If you have been over materialistic during your lifetime, such as over indulging, desire of possession or extremes beyond normality, then it will be tough going, you will not want to let go of these traits so they become your anchors to this earth.

You are required to cleanse your spirit at this time of all the dirt and grime you have collected over your lifetime from the physical world. Cleansing means removing any hate, jealousy, or prejudices you may still have and any other dross you have clinging to you. Some religions call this purgatory, but all you are doing is purging yourself of non-spiritual things, the things that cannot exist in the spirit world. The more compassionate and harmonious you have been, the easier it will be, just like having a wash after a messy job before you go for your dinner.

I would like to mention here a few sayings made by our ancestors before they passed over, things we think are funny at the time, but in all due respect have a definite meaning to them. Where they have tried to let us know what they were experiencing, but did not have the words of their vision to explain them to us. Many times ladders have been mentioned, such as Jacobs's ladder, as well as tunnels, staircases, and mountains to climb; even bridges to cross. The theme is the same of having to climb up something or other, or to cross over the bridge of no return. Then when they get to the top, they get to the pearly gates or a pair of golden gates, which is really the end of the journey and the gateway into the spirit world. Then, we get Saint Peter or some other angel checking you in. This is the individuals own interpretation of seeing a loved one waiting for their arrival, only this loved one will be so radiant that recognition is not realised until later and, of course, Saint Peter or whoever always has wings. How else would they be able to get up there to greet us, it's as simple as that. So a little more understanding of what people try and tell us, but without knowing how to do so, has come to light.

You will be able to linger here for a while in this land of paradise to get your so-called breath back, before you will have to go to what is called the hall of records or hall of memories where you will see again the whole of your life in full, unexpurgated format. You will see whether you have completed your tasks. You will see what you did— all the hidden actions you thought were untraceable— how you coped with life, how you treated others, what decisions you made or didn't make, and the effects they had on your fellow man, etc. During this judgement time, you will be able to see the effects and the emotions felt by others because of your actions, as if you were those individuals themselves. You will see how your actions were affecting them, from the point of view of your brothers and sisters. In other words, it is from the viewpoint of your fellow man. You become your fellow man for the exercise. This is a real eye opener for all those uncompassionate and cruel individuals who didn't care what they did or who they hurt in their lives. In total, you experience the entirety of all your actions and the entirety of their consequences; all your responsibilities.

Then you have to judge yourself on what you did and did not do, and there is no sterner judge than yourself. Isn't it ironic that we spend all our lives judging others, but never ourselves? And in the end it's what we are compelled to do, the only real judgement.

After you have decided your judgement, either you plan another life to see if you can correct the things you did wrong or you plan to do the things you didn't manage to do. Inaction, by the way, is just as bad in most cases as doing the wrong thing. Or, if you had a good life, did well, and accomplished your tasks, you will no doubt take a well earned break and go on from there in the ever evolving system. It will be for you to choose where to go in the future.

Now that you know what will happen to you when you pass over, if you don't like what you have done in your life up until this point of knowing, you may still have time to rectify any mishaps you have caused and change the balance. You have the chance to take the wrongs you may have done and put them right. The opportunity is yours and so is the decision; good luck to you in your quest, whatever it may be. By at least understanding the mistakes you have made, you are halfway there.

The final contact you have with the life you've just had on earth is when you return to watch your funeral if you have one. When you are prompted to attend this event, your reaction might be to say. "Haven't they got around to burying me yet? I died ages ago". That's if you are still thinking in earth time. This would make it seem like a very long time, indeed, and is caused, as you now know, by not being able to distinguish the difference between the time speeds of the two worlds. When there is no change in your own senses to this manuver, you would no doubt think this. But it should not be like that anymore, now that you know of it. Once you have witnessed your funeral and all that goes with it, for you it's off to your new or old found existence.

For those who meet a premature departure, when they are in a high state of health and living, there is only a slight difference in the transition. These tragic circumstances bring forth a set of many different, but only slightly altered views in as much as in instant death. Unless that person has seen his situation, he will believe he is still alive. It is most important that he, the victim, knows he has died. Otherwise he will linger as would a person who is trapped in his own thoughts and didn't believe in life after death. He can linger on the astral plane, just above the physical vibration of the earth, for some degree of time, wondering why he cannot move anything or feel anything solid. His hands just pass through everything he tries to touch until it then dawns on him that he is dead.

You cannot say definitely how any state of death is defined. In the case of instant death, it all depends on what state of evolution the soul of the person it has happened to has reached. We are not able to tell, we can only see the accident. The circumstances of the individual are known only to himself and all we have to be concerned about is the release of his soul. It is a sad state of affairs that the western religions rarely cater for the lost souls who do not know they are dead, when there is a simple ceremony that can be preformed for their release back to the spirit world. They just have to be drawn into the area of the ceremony, and told they are dead, and to just follow the light to find their way home. Good mediums can and do perform this service.

The most probable way an instant death is manifested in a healthy person is that he will continue consciousness right through his experience. He will feel extremely virile and energetic as he flies on through any solid objects that are in his way, being able to do anything he wishes in an instant. Knowing or sensing this, he will realise it is not natural and he will conduct himself back to the scene of the incident and see his fate, which he will recognise. The procedure is then as in all transitions to the spirit world, a journey through the black tunnel. There is no other way of dying other than being born again. It's the same, but in reverse.

Now we come to the unfortunate souls who suffered from some kind of brain disease, usually a stroke, where the person loses the ability to control themselves. All brain diseases are included in this group. The loss of the use of one's faculties doesn't alter or damage the soul of that individual in any way. In a severe case where no physical control is available or present, the mind and spirit of that person are still able to comprehend what is being said and done around their body. They are immensely frustrated at not being able to communicate with those around them and are aware that nobody understands their predicament. It is well to understand that although their body is acting in a dumb and senile way, the poor soul has lost his link with most parts of his brain. Try as he may, there is little or no response to his direction; it is most likely his autopilot has been damaged as well throwing his body works into chaos.

It is like driving along in your car with the doors all sealed up so you can't get out and all of a sudden the front wheels fall off. You are stuck and cannot move, but you still have a hold of the controls and the engine is still running, the heart is still beating. You can wave at passersby, but you are helpless to move and the engine only stops when it runs out of fuel, even when the breakdown truck takes you to the scrap yard. Unless someone is able to repair the damage, you are put in a crusher and disposed of. The unfortunate brain damaged victim is not as lucky as that, he is not allowed to run out of fuel. It is pumped into him so his engine still runs and the heart still beats. He has to endure many tests by prodding's and pokes, not to mention the embarrassments, before he finally passes on into the spirit world. The mental agony of their frustration lasts in some cases many, many months. It is indeed a happy release for them when they do eventually die. So when it comes to the loved ones who are left behind, you can rest assured that all you have said and done for them before they departed they will have heard, received, and understood to the full. Just a message to the doctors and nurses who look after these unfortunate souls, although their brain is disconnected from the control mechanism of their body, they can still feel pain and discomfort, but have no means by which to tell you. So please be gentle.

According to the ancient records, the body of the departed soul has to stand for three days before it is disposed of (buried etc). This is to allow the departing spirit to fully withdraw all of its essence that has been attached to the body during its lifetime. The parting soul can then manage much easier with the trials ahead of him, especially in regards to the raising of his vibrations to the required speed to get home.

Another very upsetting, but controversial, piece of information that has never been considered before is about the use of the death penalty and why it should not be used. When a person of bad and evil intent is executed, his spirit leaves its physical body and is then free to roam the lower astral plane, having no restrictions. He is free to influence the minds, thoughts, and actions of others and being fully charged, as you might say, from an unfinished life at the time of death, he can last in that state for years before his energies become dissipated. Even then, he can feed on the fears of those he has influenced to sustain his presence. In other words, he remains, earth bound (grounded), psychically haunting the earth plane where he is free to influence the minds and thoughts of other; weaker minded individuals here living on the earth in their physical bodies. He is able to influence them into doing more of his kind of harm. He, now being free from the restricting bonds of the physical body, can target those of similar thinking minds to do what he wants. After his experience of being caught and punished for his crime, not only would he have no remorse for what he had done, but he would be holding a grudge against his judges, the authorities of law and order, and society as a whole. The malice he holds against society he uses with great intent and can cause his thoughts and his desires to be transferred to many of the weaker minds of this world. These thoughts are then changed into action by the weaker minded victims in society. They can be from any quarter of the population and the influence he has incurred upon them degrades their standards further. They then run amok within the decent living community of law abiding citizens. This in fact is responsible for the crime waves of our civilisations. Fear not for yourself, but for the easily influenced who are so easily corrupted.

Ethically, we should be above wrongdoing from any point of view and mentally we should be alert in discriminating what is right from wrong, but that is easier said than done to someone who is having a hard time of it. These people usually pull through, though, because they have a conscience. But it is the people with no conscience who are the main targets for these begrudged entities. They are the ones who become the victims of his sort because he and his sort are attracted to this type of person. Like attracts like, remember? So persons having no conscience or safety valve in their being that would normally censer these evil thought processes would automatically think that what they have in their head is their own thought. Then they carry out what they think they thought and by doing so; activate the thoughts of the evil entity. These victims carry on the unfinished business of the dark forces without knowing or caring, but it is to their peril in the end. These wicked entities celebrate their highest delight if the victims they have influenced end up destroying themselves. This usually happens when their conscience returns and then, after they realise what they have done, they then suffer from great remorse which they can't take and commit suicide.

The soul acts like a balloon in the lower astral, only able to rise up when it has no weight attached to it. Any hate, envy, greed, etc, retained in your thoughts weighs heavily on the soul and therefore stops it from rising out of the lower aspects of that plane of existence. Until one feels any sort of remorse, no progress can be achieved.

Here again we can see where the powerful preachers obtained their story of, *hell-fire and damnation,* and the non-believers locked out of heaven. When the simple fact is that nobody can take any form of physical malice with them into the spirit world, because it cannot exist there. You are not locked out; you just have to purge yourself of all your dirt before you can enter.

Oh dear! I hope I haven't frightened anybody of the boogie-man by informing you of the lower astral plane. You have no need to worry because, unless you go hunting in dark and unholy places, or try and use the Ouija board, or are continually under the influence of alcohol or drugs that weaken the bond between your spirit and your body, these entities cannot come anywhere near you. Even if they do, for them to effect the physical plane requires a tremendous amount of their energy. So, without these aspects or help from the people who are on location at the time, who feed these ghosts by way of their fear of what they are experiencing, the entity would quickly run out of energy and fade of exhaustion. These lost souls can do damage only if you let them, by you being afraid. They can only feed on the mental energy of fear; fear is their fuel and it is as hard for them to affect us here on the physical plane as it is for us to flap our arms and fly. There is a dimension of difference between us and you don't come into contact with these beings unless you lower your standards. They can reach no higher than the lowest of the astral plane. So it is only if you get hysterical of things that go bump in the night or fear of the dark that you can hurt yourself. Just don't feed them and do what your conscience tells you; let it be your guide and leave the ghost hunting for those who really should know better and leave well alone.

Chapter 7

Some of the material you read in this book should have been given to you by the religions of the western world, but there are no present day religions in the west teaching about reincarnation, so it isn't. Yet it is taught almost as a matter of fact in most of the eastern religions. Here in the west it should be given out at all the different kinds of religions, at their churches, temples, synagogues, and all places of worship to help you understand the workings of life. It has always been thought by the authorities of the church that to give out revealing knowledge to the masses would make them lose the powers they have held for decades over the lay peoples of their domain. I presume they think that their public would no longer seek comfort or advice from them if they divulged these mysteries, in fear of the mysteries they prescribe to would no longer be mysteries. Their stories would no longer have any mystical wonderment to them. If that be the case, then they need to change their philosophy to suit. I am also presuming that most of the religions would know of this knowledge, but are fearful of the consequences if it is divulged. The question is, however, how are we going to spiritually evolve in this present draconian, unchallenged system? Especially when the answers to most of our questions are evaded by the very people we go to for the answers. They withhold them from us, or is it that they just don't genuinely know the answers themselves?

I, for one, still believe the churches provide a service of great importance insofar as the ceremonies of christenings, marriages, and funerals are concerned. They also provide a foundation for a religious enquiry to be taken on by the individual who is a seeker of the truth. Though somewhat flawed, and what isn't these days, an individual can start on a journey of a quest to find out why he is here. The scriptures are of great help to you in containing most of the information you need for your progress, but you have to sort it out. Some of it has been contaminated so don't take stories too literally. There is a quantity of misleading stories that have double and even triple meanings and, in some cases, where it was possible a miracle was thrown in to spice it up and sensationalise some of them. You also have to be aware that the whole Bible has been condensed down into what it is today and much of it is in brief. After all, the Bible has been rewritten many times and who is to stop the scribes from erasing a little bit here and adding a little bit there? Sometimes they add something of their own ideas to the age old manuscripts. Saul, who composed the Christian faith with the New Testament, comes to mind here, so you cannot rule this out. After all, it is a history book written down and recorded by scribes.

Speaking from my own point of view, especially when you take into consideration that accordingly in my previous life I had spent over forty odd years belonging to a church and studying in a Bible class, I still find myself back here reincarnated to try again. It shows, or should indicate, to you how difficult it is at the best of times to get it right and shows that maybe belonging to a church or cult is not the right way. If I hadn't have been informed of my failure, this could have meant one of five options on my return. One, I had failed my tasks in my last life. Two, I have karma to work out; three, I have more to learn; four, I returned to help my fellows; and five; I have a debt to repay. There may be more reasons, but I can't think of any at this time.

If you can't pass your tests being in the religious environment, what are we to do? It just shows you that it's just possible our church is missing the point on something, maybe on many things, and is not supplying us with the correct procedure for us to progress, although it is up to the individual to make of it what he will so he can progress. You just know there has got to be something extra that we need. It's a case, again, of our own interpretation of the written word.

We all need a starting point, a base to start from, so we should have a main religion to belong to. Even if that religion is not one's direct choice, you never know when you may need to have access to so-called holy ground and the wisdom of the clergy sometime or another to help you as you go. Christianity is not all flawed and there is some brilliant talent in our clergy it's just finding it.

I am neither out to destroy our well used system or even change it, because it provides us with a foundation, a base living code, which contains a high standard of morals and teaches us to love one another. It also gives us motivation and without motivation, everything eventually stagnates. Besides, we all need a religion of some sort or another to keep us from degenerating into a race of savages having no conscience to govern our actions. We are on that very decline in the present age, with many younger citizens not having any respect for even their parents, let alone for anyone else. Even the authorities, who are trying to uphold law and order, get in their way. Alas, respect has gone and we must get it back to be on course.

The rebels must remember that if they want to destroy the present system, they must first have some sort of efficient replacement to put in its place. Anarchy would be the result of only the one action. Most rebels don't think that far ahead and are the power possessed people who always want to be in charge. They are not prepared to live and let live. If only these authoritarians could grasp even a slight inclination that they have their own progression to consider, rather than try and disrupt as many poor devils as they possibly can, even they might get somewhere. But it is an all too familiar picture and is a scourge on mankind that frustrates everyone. Who in their right mind would want to control anyone else, haven't they enough problems of their own? But that's just it, they really have lost their minds, because by controlling others they are mounting up many problems for themselves to be answered and paid for in the process of life. They should live and let live.

We have yet to devise a system where the ordinary individual, can, after planning the amount of time his or her life span has got to last prior to returning to the earth, is to be able to actually do just this, and live out that life to the fully prescribed time that he allotted to himself. Without the chance of meeting an untimely end, like being killed or severely hampered in their business down here before they have finished. This is a major issue to be pursued in the future, although most of the decent law abiding citizens are trying to achieve this now. The only comforting consideration for being killed by the fault of someone else is that that person will inherit all your negative karma. But it doesn't help you in your quest for physical experience, so it has its drawbacks.

The highest priority for us all to face today is to obtain a system or a way that can develop our spiritual progress to the ultimate goal; that of completion of spiritual evolution on this physical plane here on earth and release from sorrow and pain. It's not an easy task now that both India and China are racing headlong into materialism and generally all the eastern countries are following suit. China, already the destroyer of Tibet, is leading the way.

Where we used to look to the east for spiritual guidance, this option is disappearing fast so we have no other choice other than to D.I.Y, (do it yourself). In the beginning that is what we had to do, so it's back to square one, although it's not as bad as that. This time, at least, we have all the information we need to help us; it can be found everywhere, you just have to know where to look. Then we have to sort it all out and discard what is not relevant to our cause. This is called the power of discrimination and is your most important sense that balances your outlook. Duplication of knowledge from different sources is a good guide and is a good indicator to the authenticity of the information gained, although it could still be flawed, so never commit yourself entirely unless you are absolutely sure of the facts. Keep the flexibility of an open mind the major factor in your search.

You don't have to, but it helps tremendously, if you study all the ancient writings of the scriptures and as much as you can find of all the new works by the modern authors of today who have researched and studied these documents, and have published the findings of their understanding of them. Besides all the other unexplained mysteries that abound in the world everywhere, the search is massive and probably never-ending. While you are doing this, you have to hold down a job and earn a living to pay your way in the world; unfortunately there are no compromises, you just have to have a determined attitude. Nothing is easy, you have to complete your daily employment and see to all the everyday chores of your life before you can indulge in your spiritual education. A point to make here is that you should not change your way of life from the course you have set yourself on, because your program is unique to you. You only need to change your attitude of mind and only then if it is wrong. So no drastic changes, life can be lived anywhere and you can still achieve enlightenment. All you have to do is take stock of what you are; who you are doesn't matter, but what you are does. It is most important to remember that.

Okay then, what is spirituality? Spirituality is made up of many virtues that can be acquired by anyone. It is not possessing or trying to possess mystical powers or any extreme activity that looks as though it gives an advantage to the individual over others. Stories of adepts who can fly or yogis who can tie themselves into knots, even those who are buried alive for many days without food or drink; all these abilities do not make anyone more spiritual. The person who attends church on a regular basis and is devoted to his faith is another false indicator because this show of faith doesn't make him spiritual; he could be the biggest rogue in the country. No, it is what you are that makes you spiritual and what you do; only you know that of yourself.

So if you are a kind and considerate person all of the time you are halfway there, because if you are those things you are not doing yourself or anybody else any harm. It just leaves the tasks you have set yourself to complete. These come in everyday situations and manifest as problems. They are repeated endlessly until you get the message to make a positive decision to stop the repetitions. This could be anything from as simple a thing as stopping yourself from gossiping scandalously about someone (very harmful towards yourself), or even, at last, taking the blame for some of the things you've done wrong, but passed the buck onto someone else saying it's not my fault. Try accepting those errors you've done or made in the past, too. Try this as well: instead of testing others on what they do, test yourself and try and see the other point of view to the argument. There are many subtle habits and actions we make every day. Some are good; some are not so good, they are just normal actions of our little ways. As long as you have consciously examined them for hidden undercurrents that could be harmful to another and have stopped those, then they are okay. Just watch for the problem you just can't seem to resolve and which keeps reappearing and raising its ugly head. They appear in differing formats, but you will know them when you say, oh no not this again! We as individuals have got to take responsibility for our actions very seriously, so that we know that any action we take doesn't interfere with anyone else's progression or cause them harm. Live the righteous way as much as you can in all that you do.

The trouble is that you can over do this aspect and it can lead into altruism, which in itself is a crime against yourself. We can be humble without being downtrodden, we can be helpful without being taken for granted, we can love without being abused, and we can be harmonious and absorb any upset. What we give out doesn't always guarantee what we will get back, not here on earth anyway. So don't be despondent if you get negative responses to what you do. You are not always responsible for other people's reactions towards you and, in any case, you cannot tell how or what another person thinks. You should never think you do know, either. A whole heap of trouble awaits you the moment you have made up your mind that you think you know what someone else is thinking. Never force your opinions onto anyone and never divulge them either, unless they are requested or they are asked for. Oh! And you don't have to suffer fools gladly; there is no accounting for fools and always fight back in self defense if you are ever attacked. Your life is very precious to you, preserve it to the last breath.

We can possess all the virtues it takes to evolve from this planet and as long as they are put into positive action when you use them, you can't do much more. Experience all you can in your life, but remember this: in your lifetime, you cannot live anyone else's life for them. You may want to help certain people and in some cases take over their responsibilities, but you can't help anybody who won't help themselves. This is advice to everybody, but is directed mainly to parents who still run their offspring's lives for them after they have reached adulthood. In doing so, you are interfering with their progress and that carries consequences. Leave your children to manage for themselves, give them their independence which you should have taught them when they were youngsters.

All this material has been leading up to the next question which is relevant to what we are aspiring to become. The question is: if you became a god and you had the planet Earth given to you as an award for your achievement, would you change things from their present format and, if so, how? Bearing in mind that all the people living here are your children and you love each and every one of them in exactly the same way, whether they are good or bad. This question is a very big teaser; most of us have our own opinions on how we would run things, it shows that you are a thinking being. But in all seriousness, how would you go about altering the unique set up here on earth, where each and every one of us has an opportunity to learn about all these different cultures around the world and then be in a position to choose the best?

The earth is such a diverse world that if you wanted to, you could go back to the Stone Age and live in the jungle. We have so many different ways of life to look at and study here, the field is enormous and the choice is yours. Our world is full of comparisons; the makeup of so many different ruling bodies gives us a wealth of material to assess. But only by studying and comparing each system will we have the knowledge to judge, which is the most beneficial. Unfortunately some of the regimes are closed or too dangerous for us and does not give the individual access to their ways of life and hidden knowledge. That goes with the job; they have to be included for the diversity.

We can't be doing too badly here in the west though, as so many eastern people, as well as others, desire to have our system of democracy, although one still wonders if there is a better way of doing things that is still not yet in our grasp. We are so readily keen on knocking what we have here in the western world without thought of what could have been, especially regarding all of our fates if we had not fought for the freedom we so proudly own today. I certainly would not have been able to have written this book. There are many oppressed countries where the people are still unable to freely express their opinions and do as they would desire.

The puzzling thing about our beautiful planet is how we have so many different coloured races of humans, yet we are all the same. We can interbreed without there being any problems with the offspring and all our destinies are exactly the same, i.e. spirituality. So if as our scientists believe, from the traces of our D.N.A., we all came out of Africa. How come we are of different colours, sizes, and build when logic tells us we should all be the same? It has been suggested that we are the leftover races from all the other populated planets of the universe that have had difficulty in progressing from the material state to spirituality. The main hurdle and major test is, for us all to be living together in harmony. What a test that is when you look around the world as it is today. They are asking for pigs to fly if that's the conclusion. I am sure most of us do not have the race relation problem, but can see the huge task ahead of convincing the less evolved of the folly of thinking there is a difference between us all. Boy, are we in a mess and brother don't we need to wakeup.

We all have to be reminded that each and every one of us has reincarnated back onto this Earth and should be grateful for a physical body that has been provided for us. We need to know that these physical bodies all work the same throughout the world, just like motorcars they also come in different sizes, shapes, and colours. There are no new souls, we just get new bodies and have to start each life we get right from scratch again. This is the most difficult dilemma that confronts us at the start of our lives and for us to cope with; it becomes so much more difficult for us when we don't get the guidance it requires to get onto the right track. The main theme in our childhood that keeps this injustice going is when we are indoctrinated into our own cultural ways of thinking so that when we become adults we are biased, instead of impartial, to all our other brothers in the world.

No wonder it takes decades to overcome these problems. We have to wait for the older, biased generations to die out before progress is made for the different ways of thinking to manifest. Then, we must again look at ourselves to make sure we are not tarred with the same outlook.

It is a true fact that example is the finest form of teaching and if somebody sets a bad example, harm is being done. We all have things we like to do, whether they be good or bad; private things. If we are truthful with ourselves, we have all been hypocrites sometime in our lives. We criticise other people's actions, then go and do a similar thing ourselves. The fact is, we learn more by making mistakes. You just try not to repeat them; it is up to the individual to make sure his bad side is not seen, especially by those who are easily influenced.

Television is one of the worst offenders of this, showing and promoting the lowest forms of humanity; trying to shock us all by the programs they sensationalise just to boost their ratings or viewing figures. Hopefully, the viewer has the power of discrimination and can see the degradation and all the things one must not do. Unfortunately, there are many small minded people who follow the trend set by these degrading programs and live their lives like it. It is of no surprise that the newspapers and televisions delight in bringing down any good person who, in their own hour of temptation, lapses from their usual high standings and are exposed as worse than just hypocrites. Even if the story proves to be untrue, they get subjected to mass coverage which destroys them anyway and in most cases is unfair. Is it right to be subjected to this one-sided, unkind treatment and then only judged on this action alone, regardless of the good they have done in the past? To be guided by the media is to prove you are fickle and easily led; your soul deserves better. Let those without fault cast the first stone.

We are drifting away from the theme of finding our way without the spiritual guidance of the eastern countries that we used to look up to for our soul enlightening journey, but who are now changing into materialistic giants, copying us here in the west. So working back to the theme in respect of us all, we must examine what we have. We all possess the asset of tolerance, which we should develop and mature so that we can share it with those whom we associate with. This helps to harmonise most aspects of our living. We must learn to accommodate into our lives other people who are attracted to us. This doesn't mean we have to give them digs or living accommodation, but just to tolerate and be kind to them; this is all that is needed to be done. By doing this, we are helping others develop their personality and at the same time expanding their minds, as well as our own. After all, the entire mind and all we know and experience is all we have when we leave the earth plane. Let me reiterate in the next few paragraphs what we are all here for, what life means to us, and the consequences of all that we do.

All of the teachings, all of the religions, and all other works that have been written on the subject of evolving of the human spirit that I have come across have all agreed on one thing and they do not differ in their conclusions. This is the statement they make, I have grossly simplified it, but in no way does it devalue what they mean: we only take with us on our death what we have accumulated in our minds during our lifetime; all and everything that we have experienced and learned while here on earth. The sum total of our being is what we know when we die, plus from all our previous lives. Some of this new knowledge will be faulty and, until the errors are recognised, they stay with you. You should have enough experience and knowledge in your mind to create your own world where you will reside until the need to move on is felt. You will be able to interconnect with all your past family and friends and add those you left behind. You will have left pain and sorrow well behind you, as this can only be experienced on the physical plane. There will be nobody from your past who you disliked, did you harm, or you didn't get on with; those persons will be on a different vibration to you, so they will not be anywhere near you. It's your world, so you decide who is with you and in it.

You are your own builder, so now you know how very important it is to get on and do your very best down here on the earth for your own benefit as well as others who will benefit from you. It goes with the saying, "the Lord helps those who help themselves, but the Lord says whatever you do will come back to you." We sow our seeds in the world of matter and we reap most of our harvest in the land of the spirit in the heavens. This world that we build is as real and as solid as the one we are living in now, but much better, more radiant with fewer, if any, restrictions. Each and every one of our worlds can be linked together to become a vast universe of spirits where we can all share in the real life after we leave the physical world. This is why we should recognise that every living soul is our brother/sister and we are all linked together in the whole of creation. There is no other way of expressing it, maybe for the want of better words we can use, "in my Father's house there are many mansions." The Lord's Prayer has a profound meaning and is conducive with most of what we require to guide us in our life here on earth today. We hear these words repeated over and over again and spoken in the churches in almost every service held in them, but we pay little attention to them for they have lost their meaning and power. This is because they are said more like a chant than a prayer, without thought, and because they are used so much they are now almost meaningless. After so long a time without thinking of what they mean, they lose their understanding as well. Sorry for sounding so much like a preacher and I don't wish to be patronising, but there is some good stuff in the Bible and it is the westerners' main guide to his salvation, so it is a good idea to read through it. It gives us the laws to follow, to keep us in order with the Ten Commandments.

The right way for the Buddhists is the middle way, a balanced journey avoiding extremes. In this they state there are four noble truths. The first is suffering, which you have to fully understand. The second is craving, which you should abandon. The third is cessation, which you have to realise; basically it means you shouldn't get attached to material things. The forth is the eight fold path that you should follow which is;

1 Right and correct views.
2. Right and correct aspirations.
3. Right and correct speech.
4. Right and correct conduct.
5. Right and correct methods of livelihood.

6. Right and correct effort.
7. Right and correct thoughts.
8. Right and correct contemplation.

So it's to lead a righteous life where possible to gain spirituality.

If you don't want to be too clever in your life by trying to become famous or trying to impress and make a name for yourself, an ambition that most youngsters suffer with in this present day and age, but a trait to be avoided like the plague, and just want to progress, you have a tried and tested method to follow. It is that of the Buddhist called "the middle way." You don't have to become one of them either to follow this principle, which should keep you on the straight and narrow, or on the right path. You don't have to go to the outer extremes of life to get to your goal, especially if you are prepared to use plenty of good old fashioned common sense as you go.

Unfortunately, our type of motivation here in the west, and now in most all parts of the world, leads us away from the required goal that everybody seeks, which is spirituality. Most everybody is involved with commercialism, competition, nationalism, idealism, religion, etc. They are all diversions from the true course the individual must take. He has to sort it out in his mind and conclude that all is not right; it is bad and in the main, immoral. All these things cause unrest, conflict, and bad feelings causing jealousy, envy, greed, sorrow, pain, but also pleasure which leads us into fear; fear of losing what we have gained. We are all preoccupied in survival and trying to avoid being ripped off or conned out of our hard earned lifestyle and possessions that has taken our hard earned effort to acquire, so we learn to trust no one. Shame on us for not allowing our better nature to shine through, but it's gotten so bad you just have to take this option. The secret is living in it, but not being of it. You have to learn to live in it because you are born in it; learn to use this system of motivation to your advantage now that you know the pitfalls. The truth of it is that there is only one way in which you can go, the one and only way, and that is to go inwards and search your soul. You have to go into your own self, into the "me" where you have all the stored answers and knowledge. The only correct way in, is to be in complete and utter silence and in isolation with no distractions of any kind. You have to be that island unto yourself and disregard that silly and famous saying which is "no man is an island unto himself." Oh yes you are, if you want to advance. We come into this world alone and we leave this world alone. We face our destiny alone and we answer to all we have done alone. Nobody can feel our pain, nobody can see into our mind, nobody knows what we are thinking when we smile or when we cry; we can hide everything we are thinking by how we make ourselves look at any time with the varied expressions shown on our faces. We are the mystery. So know yourself.

Chapter 8

This chapter is all about what other information came through during the time I was on the other side and what I was able to grasp. I will make it quite clear that I am no expert on any of the material that came to me; I can only describe what information I received. Some of it was very difficult to put into words, but I've recorded it according to my understanding and my limited knowledge. The one thing I do know is that all this material is subject to ridicule because it is not, in all due respect, what is generally accepted by the authorities and experts in their respected domains. But it is an alternative to some of the general hype and theories we have accepted without question over the years. I for one was totally amazed at what I came back with. I hope you are too.

"The human race is in a state of total AMNESIA! The present occupants of the earth cannot remember what they have been through. Every one of you has suffered death in a major disaster in some lifetime or another; there have been many of them. Blindness to the situation you find yourselves in is due to your own self destruct button and the easiness in which you accept what you are told without thought, even when you know it can't be so. Only now are you thinking of action regarding your environment. All your historic records of bygone ages have been destroyed by your fellows at certain times in the past, or they have perished in mass land upheavals. As your ancestors were of advanced intelligence and knew of the sudden displacements of this planet at certain times of its duration, they made provision for preserving the historic records and of their existence. Carved in stone and imprinted on gold and other lasting metals so it would last the eons of time, your wise ancestors made this provision so you would know of them. Unfortunately, much of the gold engraved with this history was turned into bullion and the written stone tablets were used for foundations to build dwellings. From what has been saved of these records, they have been partly deciphered and understood, but not taken seriously. Yet there are still some to be found and deciphered; these are stored in chambers and capsules around the world.

Not only do your authorities totally ignore these records, but say they are myths of the mind. They announce that you, the human race, are the only life throughout the entire universe and that life is a freak, resulting from some kind of big explosion. There is hope, however, through your technological advances. You are beginning to gain a clearer picture of how things are, so many people are slowly realising the extent of their ignorance and want to know more on the subject. They have started questioning those in high places.

It is generally accepted by most of the countries of the earth that the universe started with what you all call the Big Bang Theory. A theory it should remain. The illusion which causes this effect is the movement of the stars and galaxies. They all seem to be rushing away from, or coming towards, you. This is caused by their orbits around a centre, yes, galaxies are in orbits around a centre, but their orbits are so huge they cannot be detected from down on the earth. The centre they orbit around is then, in turn, in an orbit around another centre, adding infinitum. Another phenomenon to take into consideration is that most galaxies revolve like a wheel, from the hub to the outer edge in unison, so the stars are travelling faster on the outer edges. And by rotating like a wheel, it keeps the stars in the galaxy fixed in their positions to the earth or planet of observation, so the constellations stay the same. It is not like the solar system where the closer you get to the centre the faster you go. The illusion is set, so your view is like that from a merry-go-round. The universe is unending, but from time to time a star will burst into a huge explosion or collapse into itself. Another will be born; it goes on reproducing itself over and over again; a recycling of the old for the new.

From an explosion there comes sterility, where nothing lives. This is how things remain until there is intervention, something or someone has to intervene. Your planet was sterile until intervention took place to make it live. So why do you believe the universe started with an explosion when there would be no chance of life to begin? You well know, nothing lives from sterility. Look at your moon; even with an atmosphere it would still be sterile. Until or unless you put life there, nothing would live. You would have to intervene to give it life. Closer still, sterilise some garden soil, seal it in a container so that nothing can enter, and it will remain that way. Nothing will grow in it until there is intervention. So if it was a big bang that started it all, who could have intervened to have started it all off, when everything was sterile? But be sure that intervention took place; your question should be who?

The oldest enduring building that is still standing on the planet is the building you call the great pyramid of Egypt, a multipurpose complexity designed and built by outstanding intelligence, which still mystifies your experts. They look at it for a while then shake their heads in wonder, as to how, why, and by whom was it built? Not only was the location where it was built exactly at the centre of the landmass of the earth, it was also placed exactly on the Equator when it was constructed. This will amaze almost everybody on your planet because of its present position, but the earth's crust has moved it there! And she will move it again in the future. One of the mysteries of the earth can be explained, but like most logic will be ignored because logic threatens those in authority who do not wish to change or rewrite your history. It will certainly make them respond with disbelief at the indication of its age; to give you some idea as to how old it is, consider this: The north pole was located roughly at the centre of the country you call Alaska; some estimated 80,000 of your Earth years ago. It was during this period of time when the pyramid was build and its two companions at a place on the, then, equator. After an age of time, as expected, the earth's poles shifted in one of the greatest catastrophes recorded in the history of this planet, when it moved to where you call the Barents Sea on the Russian shoreline, a distance of some 3600 statute miles or 6000 kilometres. It has moved twice since then, from the Barents Sea it moved to where you call Hudson Bay, Canada, and on from there to its present position. It has been changing roughly every 26,000 years or so. Each time it moves, the land follows in obedience and the waters of the oceans boil over in unison to flood the land. We know this because of the pyramids. For those who believe in the rainbow promise, don't rely too much on it because you all should know by now what causes a rainbow.

The Earth's crust is in constant movement, floating on a bed of molten lava/magma, caused by the gravity stresses of the solar system. It pulls at it, creating friction, which in turn melts the rocks underneath into lava or magma. Your own scientists accept that the continents drift around, floating on molten magma, and collide with one another due to the presence of this magma deep inside the earth. At certain times, due to the unstable nature of the planet, the magnetic poles change position to another area. When this happens it has a dire and direct consequence upon the inhabitants, who can do nothing to stop it. Since the time of the pyramid's construction, it has shifted three times to where it is at the moment; because of the pyramid's present position we know all this, it tells us so. Suffice to say that it is in its most stable position now that the large continent of Antarctica is now directly under the South Pole.

Your scientists have recognised that the north pole of your planet has been in many different places, but they do not accept or recognise that this is the cause of nearly all of your planets Ice Ages. Every time the pole shifts, the area it shifts to becomes icebound. And the vacated area slowly thaws out, indicating that it had been frozen for thousands of years, which it has, but it's misleading your scientists into thinking it was an ice age for the whole planet, not just the natural Ice Cap changing its position.

When a polar shift takes place, it can move as much as fifty degrees across the globe, a distance which can be as far as 3800 miles, making the earth's crust slip over the molten magma to settle in its new position. With so much land movement, everything is destroyed, being likened to a ploughed up field. Lands are altered, they sink and rise, valleys become mountains, and mountains become valleys; little is left to show of the civilisation that existed before its movement. This is what happens, then, in a polar shift and the survivors who are left, if there are any, have to begin all over again, starting right back to the beginning living in caves; back to the caveman. And by the eons of time they take to get back to the technical standards they enjoyed and had achieved before it happened. Think of this: all their compiled, recorded history from when they started again, especially that which is passed down by word of mouth, will be to their younger generations. Old and unacceptable and will probably be believed to be as of myths and legends like it is with your world now; nothing, according to them, or you, could ever happen on a scale like that. The Earth is far too stable. Beware of your complacency, accordingly and very appropriately, your experts told you that an asteroid could never hit your planet, until a comet crashed into the planet called Jupiter and you were able to observe the resulting explosions. Those immovable scientists then altered their way of thinking, but remember, they didn't change their stubborn way of thinking, until after that collision had taken place. It would have been too late if it had hit the Earth."

I think it would be a good idea to analyse the implications of what has just been recorded here before we carry on. I have no problem with the statement about the origins of the universe that it always has been. This makes more sense to me than having the so called big bang theory. In either case, though, they cannot be proved and the question is too grand and hypothetical for us to comprehend here on Earth, but if you don't consider the alternative the scientist rules the day as he forces upon us his reasoning, so that we accept his hypotheses without having to think.

With regards to the pole shift, the information I have managed to find out is this: the earth's magnetic field is aligned roughly along the spin axis and has an approximate dipole shape, similar to that of a bar magnet, with north and south magnetic poles. This is the normal state of affairs, but occasionally the magnetic field switches polarity. The north and south magnetic poles reverse and the field settles down in the opposite state. Reversals have been documented as far back as 330 million years ago. During that time more than 400 reversals have taken place, one roughly every 700,000 years. However, the time between reversals is not constant, varying from less than 100,000 years to tens of millions of years. But the last reversal occurred 780,000 years ago. At that time, the magnetic field underwent a transition from a "reversed" state to its present "normal state." The thing is, nobody was around to see what happened to the earth at that moment.

Then there is the slow motion of the magnetic pole across the Arctic. This is due to the worldly variation of the magnetic field, a process that originates in the outer core of the earth, approximately 3000 kilometres below the surface (crust). In other words, it goes walkabouts.

What took me by complete surprise was the pyramid being on the equator when it was built. I must say, though, that it does make sense, especially after you know the reason why. All the technical data that went into the planning and construction of this monument of the past was immense and very thorough, so to place it on the equator makes for a very good reason. You don't put a building like that anywhere, and zero degrees longitude by zero degrees latitude seems just the right place.

While in this amazing dialogue of explaining the position of the pyramid, I was given a very brief glimpse at the construction site. I could see large stone blocks travelling in a line, just like a good's train pulling a load of trucks, but without the trucks or the train. There were no connections, no wheels, and no rails for them to travel along on; they were just floating above the normal ground. It was difficult to believe it was the site of the Giza Pyramids because of the greenery and vegetation of the area. I and everyone else come to that matter, are used to seeing only desert and sand. These pyramid stone blocks looked smaller to me than the ones I have seen in pictures of the pyramids, but I realised it was the size of the men who were constructing it that made the stone blocks look smaller. These men were giants; at a guess I would say they were about twelve to fifteen feet tall. On each stone block was a device that looked just like a remote control we would use for our television sets. When the stone blocks reached their allotted position, they were released in their place and the mobile devices returned, I presumed, to wherever they brought the stone blocks from.

"This pyramid was built for many reasons," continued the narration. "It was to give our scientists, the beings your ancestors called gods, information in many ways in regards to the earth. The first of many functions for this pyramid was for it to endure and last for at least one major pole shift. This would make it possible for the scientists to tell how far the earth's crust shifted when a major pole movement took place. By building it at the equator and the centre of the land mass, they had the perfect starting point to know exactly how far the land masses had moved, where it had moved to, and in what direction during the event. This had not been possible before because there had been no marker or building in a set place strong enough to survive these major upheavals. After the land masses had travelled over distances of 3000 miles or more and at a great velocity, everything had collapsed into rubble or was buried and in ruins. That is before the oceans rushed in over it all and pulverised it into unrecognisable scars on the land.

This information, of the time and movement, was essential for the scientists to know what was influencing this reoccurring major catastrophe. Each time it happened they would have to replace the livestock of the planet by gathering and collecting the different species from other Earth type planets elsewhere in the galaxy, in order to replenish the earth itself. It is time consuming as well as heart breaking for these scientists, who are the overseers of the earth and the solar system, when they see the devastation left after such an upheaval. But the eco system must be replaced for life to continue. Every living thing has its function in one way or another, the balance is essential for life to thrive. So in time, when the earth settled down, replacement then followed, and the build up of livestock began again.

Evidence of these gigantic upheavals can be found all across the extreme northern hemisphere. All the permafrost along the thawing edges of the ice line is made up of millions of crushed animals and human bones, trees, and plant life. It was where everything freestanding on the land, and otherwise, was gathered up or ripped out by the roots, and pulverised by the advancing gigantic tsunami caused by the pole shift and dropping it all at the top of the world to rot down into soil and create gas hydrates. This permafrost concoction has now started to emit large volumes of methane gas, a product of the decaying organic matter, which is what you call fossil fuel and is twenty times and more, more potent than carbon dioxide. If you asked the question, "how did the organic matter get under the ice in the first place?" your scientists and experts would be hard pressed to answer this and, no doubt, would not be giving you the answer that has just been given. With the melting of the ice sheet gathering pace, it's something else for you to worry about.

When the pyramid was completed, it was covered first in a white stone marble and then in a black material to absorb the dark rays of the sun. It would be the power source for the scientists. A sister pyramid was then constructed and covered only in a white stone marble to absorb the light rays of the sun. This gave them an alternating force, which could be used with their many devices. This power was then linked to a magnetic grid so it could be sent anywhere around the globe to specified points. The third pyramid was built as a regulator for the energy force and had to be placed slightly offline as not to interrupt the main energy flow. A fine coat of polished gold mesh was then used to cover both pyramids, the mesh allowing the sun's rays to penetrate into the pyramids with minimum loss of strength. The brilliance of the light emitting from both pyramids when this was done was blinding and could be seen far out into the solar system and far beyond as the Earth rotated in its orbit.

The effect it had was not unlike the disco dance floor lights you have, when you shine a spotlight at a globe covered in small mirrors. In the darkness you have reflected lights tracking around the walls, ceiling, and floor. Imagine this: when the bright sunlight hits the two, four sided monuments, the light reflected is so bright you cannot fix your eyes upon it. Unbeknownst to the scientists, this sent information about the earth out into space, telling any observer that there was an object rotating in a constant uniformed time span; orbiting a star in a location on the edge of a large galaxy. This had dire consequences for the scientists, the solar system, and the people of the earth.

After this signal, unknowingly being broadcast across the universe, had been active for a considerable amount of time, in that period two pole shifts had taken place. And a conservative estimate of how long, would be around 52,000 years.

Unknown beings were attracted to the solar system and were extremely warlike and had evil ways. They were red and black with tails, similar to the devils you portray in your arts. Not before time, did we find out the reason why these beings had come here, attracted via the pyramids reflections, and it was only after these beings had stripped one planet (Mars) of its atmosphere, destroying all life there, and totally destroying another planet (Asteroid Belt) that these beings were defeated. The two pyramids were stripped of their gold and all the working apparatus was removed and taken away, along with the cap stone. This was lifted off the pyramid and taken away from the earth altogether, leaving them as mysterious beacons from the past. After the removal of the capstone, erosion of the pyramid began from the top downwards and has continued to the present day.

To our dismay, these red beings have left a legacy with the people of your planet. Because of the contact they made with the peoples of your world, horrendous violent fighting, affording no mercy, took place here. You have inherited their warlike nature, which has delayed your progress. This trait cannot be extinguished from your being, it has been absorbed into your makeup and only the people of the earth can eradicate it from their souls. There is no other way in which it can be done. Not until you are able to subdue this affliction and eradicate it from your nature will you be able to enter your next stage of development and progress on the evolutionary path. This was also the major factor with the scientists, the overseers, breaking their contact with the peoples of the earth. No longer do they dwell among you, not for over 3,000 years. A word of advice here for all the non-violent souls, you must not confuse self defense with aggression. Self defense is not aggression and must be used at all times to preserve the freedom of the individual. Every man has the right to protect himself and to live his life to the full; to the full time span that he has allotted to himself before he reincarnated. This is what humanity must strive for; that every human being can live out his or her allotted life span in peace, without interruption.

Some considerable time after the completion of the pyramids, the event of the earth's pole shift occurred. Although the movement of travel of the pyramids was over some distance of 3,600 miles, there was little damage, if any at all, to them. We put this down to the rock base foundation where they were situated. Elsewhere, in the cities and where there were buildings, total destruction was observed. Nothing was left in the direction to which the trail of the poles took. It was utter and complete destruction of everything that was once there. At the two pivotal points where the land was less affected, where you would expect to find survivors, they in turn were washed away, except for those on very high ground. This particular pole shift was extremely vicious, leaving nothing and burying most of the high civilisation that existed at the time. Two more pole shifts occurred before the present period where they stand in the desert today. In the previous pole shifts, the pyramids were partly submerged, and before that at the time when they were built, the land enjoyed equatorial weather with monsoon type rains to nourish the land.

Now we had the starting point of the trouble. It seems that the triggering point to the pole shift movement is when the earth reaches the nearest point to the sun in its orbit. That would be several days after the winter solstice of the northern hemisphere and at the same time when the moon is new or between the earth and the sun, a solar eclipse. Although this was not the major cause, it was the trigger. This became a very important event in the calendar of the human race; in fact it became an obsession. Stone monuments were built for the purpose of telling exactly when this solar eclipse would take place, so at least the people could be prepared. Solar eclipses, especially total, were feared. Even now, they are awesome to you. Over the course of time, when the non event syndrome kept occurring; that is, nothing happened when it was expected to, the fear of the people subsided. The memories through the ages started to turn into the stories from long ago. The reason for the monuments was eventually lost, the understanding for what they were for had been forgotten and their uses changed. Different meanings by different tribes made them a religious attraction. All sorts of ceremonies took place, even sacrifice, but underneath all this ceremony was an inborn feeling in all of the people that these monuments meant something, something of great importance. Anyone who goes to look at them gets this feeling, no matter who they are. The stone monument called Stonehenge was severely damaged in the last pole shift. This means its well over the age your experts say it is, but everything that your experts date has to be after what they think was the last ice age. They cannot comprehend anything older, as they believe civilisation only started about 6,000 years ago when everybody came from the caves, from the Stone Age; where you all go after a pole shift, back to the Stone Age. Each and every one of the human race has all this information stored in their subconscious, they have been there before. It is the total AMNESIA you all suffer from that prevents these recollections from surfacing. All your science fiction stories have a foundation from past events. The author is only recalling from deep within his soul memories of what has been before."

* * *

That is about it. It is enough to send shivers down your spine. We now have to sort this material out and put it into acceptable contexts, go through it, and find some sort of backup if we can to answer a few of the many questions. My first concern is in not knowing the main factor of what causes the poles to shift and the second is when is it due to happen again?

I went on the Internet yet again and typed in solar eclipse, and was directed to Eclipses Online Portal. It gives you an animated view of any solar or lunar eclipse from the year 1501 to 2100. I found that the annual eclipse for the time we require is from January 2nd 1508 and from there on after that roughly every eighteen to nineteen years. The next solar eclipse that would be of interest in this case is January 4th 2011, or in the same year December 24th 2011, a year before the often referred to Ancient Mayan calendar, which runs out on December 22nd 2012. There is no new moon near that day, so you don't need to get all gloomy. I think the end of the Mayan calendar is not signifying the end of the world, as a few authors have suggested, but is signifying the end of the Age of Pisces and the start of the Age of Aquarius, although I could very well be wrong.

The main function of this book though is not to solve the problems of the earth, although we can have a go, but to create the desire in the reader to spiritually evolve and gain enlightenment; to break the cycle of forever returning to this physical world of suffering and pain with very little pleasure so you don't have to return here anymore. Some of the keys to do just that have been given in this book. But before we leave a very questionable situation that I have reached in this chapter, I will give you three pieces of information to stimulate the enquiring mind on the last subjects: a theory on crustal displacement, the end date of the Mayas of December 21st 2012, and why the Sphinx was created.

It has been suggested that approximately 12,000 years ago there was a displacement of the earth's crust. The entire outer shell of the earth moved approximately 2,000 miles. When the earth's crust shifted, all of Antarctica was encapsulated by the polar zone. At the same time, North America was released from the Arctic Circle and became temperate. This corresponds to the North Pole shifting from Hudson Bay to its present position. Thousands of animals were found to be frozen in a brief moment in time in the northern hemisphere. This theory is based on the theory of continental drift. This is possible because the outer crust of the earth floats upon a semi-liquid layer. The theory of crustal displacement states that the entire crust of the earth can shift in one piece, like the loose skin of an orange.

December 21st 2012, the end of the Mayan calendar, is a conjunction of the winter solstice with the sun crossing our galactic equator. This is a very rare event indeed, which takes thousands of years to manifest, approximately once every 25,600 years. It's incredible that the Mayans knew about this event, but they got their knowledge from somewhere. On this particular day, the South Pole will be pointing towards the centre of our galaxy and for the next few weeks after. Hopefully, the South Pole won't be altered or disturbed in any way.

If it is disturbed, you must remember that we are eternal beings and cannot be destroyed. We have always existed and have been through it all before, but this time we will try to remain conscious throughout so that it can be experienced. If you do not survive in your physical body and it is destroyed, don't despair. If you can remain conscious, you will find that you will carry on regardless of what happens. You will be able to watch the event to its completion, even to watching what happens to your physical body. So don't close your eyes, don't faint, and don't fear because you cannot change your fate. Witness everything you can and learn. Watch the power of natural occurrences that helped to shape the earth. You are forever, remember this. If you survive in your physical body, you are to carry the banner and make the bodies, for the next civilisation, for us all to be able to come back and finish our lessons. But I don't think we have that to worry about yet, there are other things to be completed here on this Earth first before a major event like a Polar Shift takes place.

If the information I have received is accurate, and I have understood it and explained it all correctly, then our planet has travelled around and through the twelve constellations we can see in our galaxy three times since the building of the Great Pyramid. During that period the Earth's crust has been displaced three times also. If the earth takes, on average, 26,000 years to complete one circuit of the constellations or one Earth wobble (this is not an orbit of the galaxy), then on average we have one polar shift each wobble (26,000 years). If this is so and the last polar shift happened around 12,000 years ago, we are not due for any unforeseeable disruptions on that kind of scale for another 14,000 years or so. Don't let this information make you any less aware of what might happen in the future, though, owing to the instability of our planet. But if you backtrack those 12,000 years, it takes us back to the constellation of Leo the lion. Is it not just a coincidence that our ancestors, who have been painstakingly leaving us messages for our wellbeing over the centuries, would carve out the figure of a lion from a solid piece of rock facing east and the dawn of each day, looking for what is to come, i.e. looking into the future, waiting for his constellation to come again? Even then, carving it out in front of the pyramids that gave them so much information on the deluge catastrophes. They are telling us in the only way it was possible for them to leave a message so it would survive and outlast the destruction of time, knowing everything is destroyed when the catastrophic polar shift takes place, hoping we will understand what they are trying to tell us. It seems they were also preparing for their possible return as well; after all they are our ancestors.

Just put that way of thinking into your mind for a moment and you will see the message. The last polar shift took place in the constellation of Leo the lion. The Sphinx was carved out of solid rock before the last polar shift to survive the catastrophe and tell us so. When it was first carved it was that of a lion, but due to the massive ego of one of the pharaohs, the head was changed from a lion to his face. You can see this from the dimensions of the head, which is now a lot smaller than it should be and is far less eroded than its body. You may wonder why this could be when the body has been protected by the prolonged coverings of the desert sands, so it should be the other way around with the head suffering more erosion than the body. Its great age is made obvious by the erosion caused by water, indicating a different climate when constructed and is a sure sign that it was while the earth was in the process of passing through the constellation of Leo that the fateful polar shift took place. It also tells us that it was for the second time since the carving of the Sphinx. The fact about the very ancient age of the Sphinx is arrived at by remembering that the sand collected around the Sphinx and kept it buried for long periods of time, therefore protecting it from erosion. We are told the pharaoh prince, Tuthmosis the fourth, cleared away the sand before repairing it way back some 3500 years ago. Then it was done again in Roman times, then again by Captain Caviglia in 1818, again sixty-eight years later by a Gaston Maspero, and lastly again in 1925. Since the last polar shift it has been mostly under the sands of the desert with only the head showing above the sand, so the water erosion must have been before the last deluge. All sorts of labels have been given to the giant Sphinx from the very start of the present historical time for this age of the human race. It has always been there and no one knows what it was for, so past historians have invented a whole chapter of reasons for its existence. Now if the Sphinx had been carved out and created in this time zone, we would have a recorded memory of just that. Even by word of mouth we would have had at least a corresponding myth, but because it has always been there we haven't, so doesn't this speak for itself? Well, we have just solved the riddle of the Sphinx and should give our ancestors a little bit more credit. They knew way back then that they would be reincarnating back onto this world some time or another after these events had taken place and it was in their interest to leave some kind of clue to what had happened in the past. Don't we all at this present time make plans for the future? We are now those people, our ancestors back on earth, and they had the means at their disposal then, to leave a lasting message to be recognised by us, thinking we would be bright enough with our numerous reincarnations back to this world to recognise the signs, hoping just one of us may remember one day what it all meant. Maybe that would not have happened just yet due to our present way of thinking, with the Egyptologists blocking the way. Had it not been for my near death experience gaining this knowledge, the question is, "would I be thinking this way at all, had my experience not occurred?" The answer to that is very unlikely. Even now, this information may not be accepted, but I hope it will be. At least it has been recorded, written down for future reference for someone else to take it up. Who knows, but be sure not to let yourself get possessed with an over inflated ego like almost all the politicians, scientists, and all those people who make up the authority these days. They stop progress, so you must watch your motive too. You must rely on your own judgement in cases like this because, in truth, the authorities do not know. They only have the old, outdated theories that they preach non-stop to us, the public. And now we have a better understanding of the sciences, etc. They are struggling to keep ahead of us.

We are all inflicted with this terrible feeling that we are all going to die in a sudden disaster, the inbred part of us knows that it's happened before. It doesn't surface very often, but when it does I hope this will give you a little comfort and stops the worry you would otherwise have endured. We are about to enter the Age of Aquarius. Aquarius is the opposite constellation sign to Leo, which could be a little worrying. In other words, it is the opposite side of the coin, heads or tails, it's your call.

All the modern writers who are involved with the investigation and answers to the mysteries of the Great Pyramid at Giza (excluding most of the Egyptologists) may have had a hand in its development all those years ago. They may have a weak memory block so that something is getting through on the subject. There is an instinct within all of them that tells them the present accepted theories are all wrong and they need to be totally rethought. The most suspect information on the subject comes from a Greek called Herodotus and not an Egyptian. How bizarre is that? Guess who subscribes to his version, yes, the Egyptologists, yet they dismiss Plato's account of Atlantis.

Now to finish off the chapter, I would like to look at a couple of niggling problems I have with the Great Pyramid at Giza. In the narration, the information given was that the cap stone was lifted off and taken from the Earth. After reflecting on this, I came to the conclusion that it was probably the only way possible to remove it other than blowing it off with cannon fire or explosives. I say this because have you ever tried to walk up a 1 in 4 gradient? That is a slope or hill that rises in height one foot in every level length of four feet. While on this gradient have you tried to manuver something such as a bicycle, or pushchair, or even a backpack. You will find it is somewhat difficult. Bearing that in mind, now compare that to the gradient of the Great Pyramid which rises 1.25 feet in 1 foot; that represents a rising slope of five feet in only four feet of level ground. You can see that you would not be able to even stand up or climb at such a gradient, let alone be able to carry out any form of manual activity. So even if you think that it was possible to push the cap stone off of the top of the Great Pyramid, you are talking of a feat that manually is an impossibility. It is stated that the summit of the second pyramid is inaccessible because of its remaining few casing stones around the summit. The reason the Great Pyramid can be climbed at all is because all the casing stones have been removed, the Egyptologists say they were used to build most of the nearby city of Cairo. Without the original casing stones, it has allowed access by means of the large blocks now exposed, providing a type of stairway up to the top with a flat area of over thirty square feet. It is also presumed by the Egyptologists that the cap stone was made of one complete block of stone, probably granite, and represented one percent of the Pyramid; being an exact duplicate of the Pyramid in miniature. If this is so, it would have weighed twenty odd tons or more. It is also believed it was keyed into the pyramid, fat chance of pushing it off then. Whatever you may think, the cap stone has never been found and will remain one of the most mystifying problems that belongs to this magical monument. Because of the erosion from the top, we have a missing height space of twenty-seven feet to account for. It was 480 feet high and it is now reported to be 453 feet high. If you take into account that the cap stone was probably about twelve feet high, we still lose fifteen feet of stone. I've put it this way simply because a twenty-seven foot high capstone would have been enormous and not in proportion to the one percent of the pyramid.

There are no records of anybody ever seeing the capstone in place on top of the pyramid or where it even could be now. There are no records of anyone ever seeing it at all. If the pyramid has existed for that enormous amount of time and survived the catastrophes mentioned in the previous chapter, while all human life has failed to survive from these catastrophes, then I am not surprised. The same applies to the pyramid as that of the Sphinx; that it has always been there throughout our history. But it would be nice to know what material the capstone was made out of or consisted of, was it granite, clear crystal, silver, or gold? For a monument constructed with such precision, nothing less would have done. It was covered in an estimated 144,000 casing stones carved to fit exactly onto the blocks underneath. They weighed over fifteen tons each and were cemented together with a mortar no thicker than a piece of paper. This mortar was stronger than the stones themselves and was of an unknown origin. It has been analysed and, although the chemical composition is known, it can't be reproduced. Some of the joints were so perfect it was hard to tell if there was a join there at all. Initially after the five chambers above the King's Chamber were opened, the people that had entered the second chamber were turned black by a powder that existed only in that chamber. This powder was analyzed and it was determined to be the dust from the castoff shells and skins of insects, a mystery within itself. There must have been billions and billions of them to create so much powder and why only in the second chamber? And how long would it take to amass so many insects and then for them to break down into powder? The questions keep pouring in with no qualifying answers. There is no way in our modern times that we could ever build such an accurate building, so how can we answer the question of how was it built and by whom? It is what you would call an OOPO's (out of place object) and an embarrassment to the know-all historians who woffle on about slaves and avoid the delving and probing questions.

A watermark of encrusted salt about halfway up the pyramid shows that it was once under the sea. This puts its date of construction back before 10,000 B.C., when all that area was under the Mediterranean Sea. Now that makes you wonder, but don't accept my word for it. Find it out for yourself; the information is there to be found. Don't rely on the Egyptologists for your information though, as they are not prepared to modify any part of their beliefs with any new relevant information. They still believe it was a tomb, built by thousands of slaves pushing and pulling the stone blocks on wooden rollers and carving the granite blocks with soft cooper chisels. There again, they make the mistake of thinking life started only 6,000 years ago and limit themselves to any more progress on the subject with this closed minded attitude. Because they are the so called experts and are also the authority within this field, no one is allowed to intrude. It is a big case for the inflated egos brigade and the, we know best type; anyone who suggests anything different other than their strict hypothesis is called a pyramidiot. Well, at least, a pyramidiot doesn't belong to the flat earth society.

However hard we try to unfold the mysteries of our past, unless we change the way we think, our progress stops. Every time we try to solve a mystery from our past, we get the problem of being handicapped by the way we have been educated. Unless we change the way we were taught to think, our problems remain. We are all taught a massive lie while we are at school that clouds our outlook for the rest of our lives. That lie, along with a few others, is that the history of our civilisation started around 6,000 years ago and there was nothing before that. This is pure poppycock, yet the authorities insist on teaching us this as a fact, but it is only a theory. What is more amazing about it, though, is it is contradictory to the theory of evolution. You can't have them together because it is absurd, but here again they teach and promote them both. They teach and promote Darwin's theory of evolution and tell us we all came from apes, to add to the confusion. Until such evidence of us changing from ape to man is found, it remains a theory. Darwin's theory is nothing more than a hazardous guess accompanied with a very convincing hypothesis in the study of species. There is no evidence that any species, whatever it may be, has changed into anything else other than its own kind. Alterations' occurring to any known species has never happened and has never been found anywhere. If you cross a horse with a donkey, you get a mule or a hybrid which is sterile and cannot reproduce. It is the same in any cross breeding; the offspring is always sterile and cannot reproduce without the interference of science. No interbreeding has occurred between animals, birds, reptiles, or insects and there is no in-between species that we can see developing now nor in the archaeological finds of the past. A good example of this is my own observation during my life while fish keeping. The two fish species I refer to are the Roach and the Rudd, they are almost identical fish. They live together, they shoal together, but they never interbreed. Each is a pure replica of its own kind, there are no in-betweens. This goes for all natural life that has not been interfered with by man. So always keep an open mind with no commitment to any theory while it remains a theory. In other words, don't accept anything you are told without there is a backup or a logical explanation to it. Any doubt should remain reserved within oneself until cleared to your own satisfaction. And here is why you should do this, reason this as possible if you can: take two tons of iron ore, half a ton of coal, twenty gallons or so of seawater, and add what you think might help. Mix them up, wait two million years or so, and you should, according to our evolutionists, get a Rolls Royce motor car or similar. That is what you are expected to believe in a parallel case involving our own evolution. There is a slight problem here, though, and has to be taken into account. That is, the human body is a far more complex and sophisticated in comparison to that of a car, so it may take a little longer to appear. You have to decide about this, after taking into account the kind of things you have been taught and led to believe and because it is your choice.

Chapter 9

Logical and illogical statements and material contained in these pages and elsewhere, for that matter, may never be analysed sufficiently to everyone's satisfaction. An understatement would be to say that this book contains, to some degree, illogical information to the average man and oh dear, there is more to come. All this information should be, quite acceptable to our physical predicament if only we let down the materialist barrier we cling to so tightly. We should try and analyse all that we can with what we know. Things are happening all the time that cannot be explained, things that are not logical. It is up to us to apply the logic where we can. We must not dismiss things that do not fit into our world and cannot be explained. If they are there, then we must try to solve them and end the mystery without the so called experts telling us differently, who respond with some stupid, dreamt up explanation that deepens the problem still further. I find some of the explanations given out by the experts quite fascinating and some of them are really funny and way out, sometimes more way out than the mystery.

We have a good example here of a point missed and an explanation in a recent reported story as follows, it was thought very funny at the time, but the point, as I said, was missed:

Friday September 14th 2007— A Czech speedway rider knocked unconscious during a race woke up speaking perfect

English. Matej Kus, 18, could barely speak a word of English before coming off his bike and have another rider drive over his head, splitting his crash helmet. He was out cold for forty-five minutes, then came round and asked paramedics where he was and what had happened in a posh English voice. Stunned team boss Peter Waite said, "He sounded like a newsreader. He was speaking perfect English without any sort of accent."

He lost his memory for forty-eight hours and as soon as it returned, he lost the ability to speak English. Back home in Pizen, in the Czech Republic, he said through an interpreter, "There must be some English deep in my head, but obviously I needed a bang on the head and a crash for it to come out. Hopefully I can pick some English up so I'll be able to speak it without someone having to hit me over the head."

Doctors say he suffered from the extremely rare Foreign Accent Syndrome caused by a stroke or a blow to the head which damages the parts of the brain that control speech—.

Little snippets of news like this are rarely noticed and are seldom reported. This one was because it was somewhat of a novelty, but the implications are far reaching. There are ways of explaining away things like this, as the doctors, did above so that no other thought is given to it, but I think reports like this deserve a better explanation. I think it is a case of this man's brain losing its link with his mind for that time period which allowed his subconscious to be accessed. The mind then linked up again with his brain on recovery and, being slightly confused and mixed up over the knock on the head, revealed the knowledge gained from a previous life. I don't know about you, but I still find it difficult to pronounce new words I come across now and again in the English language, besides some I already know. In this case, the mind of this young man worked his brain with remarkable skill from the wealth of knowhow and experiences of his memories. It also gives us a kind of proof of a past life and also in reincarnation.

Here is another little snippet of news concerning our subject reported January 2008:—

Twins separated at birth and adopted by separate parents later married each other without realising they were brother and sister. The pair were granted an annulment after a High Court judge ruled the marriage had never validly existed. The identities of the British pair and details of the relationship and marriage have been kept secret. But it is known that they were separated soon after birth. They were never told they were twins. They did not discover they were blood relatives until after the wedding. The case was uncovered by Lord Alton in a conversation with a High Court judge. He used it to highlight perceived deficiencies in the Human Embryology and Tissue Bill, currently going through Parliament.—

Now here is an example of two souls coming back to the physical plane and wanting most desperately to be together during their time on Earth because of their undivided love for each other, and not wanting to be separated. They probably thought that because they were being born as twins they would always be together, not taking into consideration that life kicks up many surprises and uncertainties for us all down here on Earth. I hope they progress together after this unhappy hiccup and it hasn't affected them too dramatically, but wow! How about that, finding one another against all the odds and after such a terribly long separation, it just goes to prove that like attracts like and the stronger the bond, the more powerful the attraction. Their vibrations were so attuned that hell and high water couldn't keep them apart. This type of news is a rarity, but a booster to all of us who are searching for answers. Be on the lookout for more of these snippets of news, you never know what you might find.

Let us then explore the range of vibrations that our physical senses can detect for us that let us know what is about us in the physical world. It is an interesting subject because vibration is everything and without vibration we cannot exist. There is a wide range of vibrating matter that we live in and we presume that we are in the middle of this frequency range while it extends out to what seems to us as being our extremes, that of the high and low and the far and wide. We call it the third dimension, so anything that is in the third dimension we should be able to sense in some way. We can sense things through the vibration detectors that our bodies have been equipped with, which give us some idea of what exists around us in this third dimension. Through our flesh and the courtesy of our nervous system, we get the sense of feeling and we use our fingers when we need to touch any object to know its texture, etc. With our tongue we sense taste, with our nose we sense smell, with our ears sound, and with our eyes sight; our windows to the world. Each of these senses has a limited receiving range of these vibratory frequencies from low to high and from narrow to wide, like the wave band on a radio set picking up the signals transmitted by radio stations on different frequencies. In fact, that is just the way it works. We live in a frequency wave band in which there are millions upon millions of them all vibrating at a different speed.

Our five physical detecting senses are receiving the vibration frequencies of objects made up of matter that are all around us in our three dimensional world. We can detect only a minuscule part of the massive vibration range that makes up the living cosmos. What we call speed is the general governor of all that we sense. All these things are existent through a constant rate of vibration set at a unique frequency or speed for each and every particular form. If you look through a microscope at any object, it will appear quite different to the normality of the thing viewed, but if you keep increasing the magnification it changes out of all recognition. Microorganisms can appear as monsters, but if you keep increasing the magnification they, in turn, disappear. You can see right through them because they become too large to see. Increasing the magnification, you eventually arrive at the famous molecule, the building blocks of our material plane, the physical world. Going further on down, we get to the atom; further down to electrons and protons, to quarks, etc. Further on down the scale is where the carbon elements are fused together by the DNA patterns that construct these molecules into different objects of matter. Each construction, having a different code and vibratory rate than the other to define what it will be, this is where the miracle of our physical and material bodies are created. For us to occupy and use, including all the other forms and material we observe through our five known senses that detect the different and varied things of our vibrating physical world. You can see now why radiation and microwaves are very dangerous to us, as they can interfere and alter the patterns of our material make up.

If you were to shrink down inside yourself far enough and became so small as to be able to live on one of your electrons orbiting an atom, as if it were a planet, and you looked up, your body would appear to you just like the universe that we all see looking up in the sky on a clear night, viewing from the Earth. It is a thought for us all to ponder over and wonder about, especially with the time difference with you being so small; a prospective to bring you understanding if you care to allow it.

To us, the slowest of our sense range is feeling. The most noticeable aspect of that sense is when we feel either, hot or cold, cold being the higher rate of speed, believe it or not, of the two extremes. But it is wise to just keep warm and stay in the comfort zone, because both extremes are unhealthy to the physical body. There is a whole range of different material that we can sense through our fingers and flesh, from sensing metal, stone, wood, and cloth up to living animals, etc. The sensations of feeling are multiple, from extremely pleasurable to downright horrific.

Moving up the scale to our next sense, we come to taste. The sense detector for taste is the tongue, which is also very sensitive to the first sense of touch. As we know full well, if you put something very hot or very cold into your mouth, you can damage the taste buds on your tongue and put them out of action for a few minutes or more before they return to normal. The tongue is also involved in forming different sounds, but the main function is taste. The taste frequency range starts from downright vile, on to bitter, through to savoury, and on to sweet and a whole host of in-betweens that you care to concoct. The number of different tastes that can be experienced within the vibration range is amazingly large. There is a taste for nearly everything, or should I say, everything has a taste, including none foods.

Going on up the frequency scale to the next sense, which is very close to taste, we come to smell. The link is so close you can almost taste some smells. The nose is our detector of smells and some smells can be very powerful, not only in strength to hurt the sense detector and make your eyes water, but in awakening your memory cells to events you can associate with from the past, although, you can say this for all the senses. Here again we have a massive range of odours and yet it is remarkable how limited we are in this sense. You only have to watch a dog to know this limit. He can detect smells from either end of the scent scale that we, with our limited range, would never detect or imagine existed; when you see this for yourself it is amazing. My experience with this was with my own dog, a crossbreed between a Springer Spaniel and a Golden Retriever. I used to throw a hard rubber ball around the garden for him to retrieve. Many times he lost sight of it, but found it by his sense of smell and the scent of the ball. Now and then I would trick him into thinking I had thrown it for him and, while he was running from me, I would place it in a bucket of water. After a few minutes of searching, he would inevitably find it and it never ceased to amaze me.

Dogs are not the only animals to have a greater range in the sense of smell than a human does and it is an indication of how wide the frequency the sense of smell has. This is the case, in fact, with all of our senses in as much as we are limited to only a small window on the scale of each frequency. Here is a little tip if you ever need to pick up a very faint or weak smell, or you need to increase the strength of your smell sense for a moment. There is an old Indian trick of breathing in and out through your nostrils very rapidly for about seven or eight times. When you have done this, you will find it makes the inside of your nose very tender, but you will have heightened your sense of smell for a few moments. You can see animals in the wild do this when they feel there is danger around or when they are hunting for their prey. So now you know why they raise their heads and look like they are twitching their nostrils.

The closeness of the senses becomes more apparent when we get to our next sense, which is hearing, where our ears are the detectors of sound and sound is a major player in the vibration stakes. We can even feel the vibration of sound, although without our ears it has no variety of tone whatsoever. So to appreciate any form of sound, we need our ears to pick up the different vibration rates of the sound wave forms, starting from way down low to pitching very high, until we eventually cannot hear anymore, The notes have gone out of our limited frequency range and we can no longer detect any sound at all, whereas animals are still able to pick up such signals. This is one way of realising that just because you cannot hear, see, smell, taste, or feel something with your senses, it doesn't mean to say that there isn't anything there. To us, there are many unsolved mysteries only because we have limited resources within our physical makeup and unless we are prepared to take into account this major defect, we are not going to advance very far. Sound is a vibration that can move the emotions, physical objects, make the hairs on the back of the neck stand on end, and has power of immeasurable strength. We can raise our vibrations by listening to music that is to our own liking, the liking indicates that the music is compatible to you and makes you feel good, but may not have the same result for others. There are some pieces of music that inspire thousands of people just by being played. By this I do not mean national anthems or music you have been subjected to for long periods of time, because these are indoctrinated into us, some at birth or at other times in our lives and are not of our choosing. This is not the type of music I mean. When you think about this, personal choice is what I am referring to; when you hear a piece of music for the first time and you are able to actually listen to it, you can then tell instantly whether you like it or not, not after you have been bombarded with it for several weeks. Music you personally choose raises your vibrations, but maybe not somebody else's, so it is a good idea not to enforce your choice without maybe some sort of communication with your listeners first.

Musical sound attracts different people, young or old, into varied categories depending on the type being played. The music you prefer is sure to raise your vibration, but other types can depress or even drive you to distraction. The sounds that you hear are made up of the eight different notes and are repeated an octave higher and so on until they disappear from our sense of detection. When these notes are put into a pattern of order and played one after the other or together in harmony, this gives you music and, if put in the right sequence for your pleasure and to match your vibration, can lift your spirit. If it is played in disharmony, it can result in agony. The next time you hear a jet engine, you are listening to all the known notes and all their octaves played at the same time, creating the noise that blasts from the jets exhaust. Here you can hear the power of sound.

The sound scale is the best example in explaining how all the vibration scales work, as it demonstrates how you go from low to high by moving up a series of notes represented by the black and white keys on a piano keyboard, the higher the note, the faster the vibration. To finish the sound vibration, a last fascinating observation on music, have you noticed how each different country has its own type of music? If you were to listen to each different kind, I wonder which one you would like the best. Without being bias, we tend to like the music that we have been brought up with, but, is it the music you really like?

Our last physical sense is sight and, light is the next highest vibration along and up the scale. Our eyes not only pick up vibrations from objects of all different kinds, we also perceive colours and movement. Our eyes can hardly detect objects in the dark unless these objects are radiating their own form of light, like glow worms and fireflies. They are luminous and are independent of light and are able to be seen without the help of light. But if it is pitch black darkness, we can't see at all. Again we have been short changed in this department, unlike the animals who are able to see without the aid of light, especially the cat that has the capacity to see ghosts. If we were able to see as the cat does, there would be no need for us to search for proof of life after death because we would be able to witness the passing of our loved ones at the moment of death. We could watch their spirit leaving their body and be able to follow their short journey in the lower astral plane until such time as to when they had finally lifted their vibrations above that of the Earthly physical and Earthly lower astral planes and gone up out of reach of all Earthly and physical senses. If we were able to watch and see this then, as I said before, no proof would be needed for life after death. So the animal has the upper hand regarding sight, with few exceptions. Here again I bring you proof of sight in the darkness via an animal. When I have thrown my dog's ball for him in pitch black darkness, he has the same skill as if it were daytime, he has no trouble in finding and fetching it. His sight was as if it was in daylight, but most animal owners will know and vouch for this.

The colour spectrum is another way to describe how the scale of vibration works, as all vibrations change with speed and also alter with temperature. The colour scale is shown to us in a rainbow, which obviously needs light rays for the colours to manifest. You can see that they start with red, which is the slowest vibrating colour and slow enough for you to see on rare occasions when it manifests for a split second from a very loud sound. This shows that some sounds get very close to sight, by manifesting a colour. This, though, depends entirely on how the individual manages his senses and whether he has been gifted with ESP (extra sensory perception) or has raised his vibrations sufficiently enough to get this extra treat. Orange is the next colour up on the scale, followed by yellow, green, blue, indigo, and violet in that order. Succeeding the violet and further increasing the vibration speed gives pure white, further and faster gives a grey, and our sight hits its limit when we get to black. Black, to a certain extent, is the gateway to other dimensions. In the case of the black holes in space, they are vibrating at a higher rate than that of physical light, so they cannot emit any. Black or darkness is what we fear the most because we cannot see anything or know what is going on.

We can go on up the scale a little further where our senses combine together to sense electricity. We know it is there, but we cannot see it because with a further speed increase to our sight sense, it has overtaken our sight limit so we no longer detect it. Light is followed, according to our senses then, with electricity and on up to psychic force and then onto the lower astral plane. It is possible to see a ghost with our combined senses, but this is the limit of our physical capabilities. If you want to reach higher, then you have to seek metaphysical assistance or die to the physical plane, unless you are a cat of course.

Maybe we should allow a word on this matter of vibration from the famous scientist Albert Einstein, because everyone believes what Mr. Einstein says, whether he is right or not. He tells us that—

"Physical matter is nothing more than a concentrated field of force, what we call physical substance that makes up solid objects. Everything we see in the three dimensional world that we call matter is in reality an intangible concentration of wave forms of vibrations. Different combinations of all these structural patterns of these waves of vibrations unite together to form the millions of chemicals and elements that in turn react with one another to form physical substances of different things. Different wave forms of this matter appear to us to be solid because we are made up of similar wave forms that vibrate within a clearly defined range of frequencies. And we live within this frequency band which controls the physical processes of our limited three dimensional world."

So there you go, even Albert Einstein had a go at explaining the makeup of our physical world.

Electricity is the next vibration up the scale from light and is a vibration we all like to think we understand. Unfortunately, we cannot understand it properly because of not having the specific sense to see it. According to speed, this is the next vibration up the scale from light (sight), but electricity, what is it? We know it is there; we use it in our daily lives, we can store it in batteries, and we think we make it through generating it. Okay, we generate it, but where does it come from in the first place to get into the generator? This has not been solved or thought about because the simple reason is that we take it so much for granted. Why bother to find out where it comes from when it's already there for us? By thinking this way, we miss the opportunity to make any advancement in this field. The only answer I can come up with, and is a kind of theory of mine, is that it is part of the makeup of the atmosphere of the Earth. And it acts just like the properties of water. To explain what I mean about this theory, although I should really say it is an idea as I am not in any way a scientist and only scientists are allowed theories. So how I see this idea is explained as follows:

Electricity is seized from the atmosphere by a generator or dynamo. Electricity, in its natural state, is evenly spread among all the other elements that make up the atmosphere and in that state can be called Aether (ether). This Aether is similar to, or equivalent of, the eastern name of Prana. When it is condensed and concentrated down, it turns into electricity, but in so doing loses its life-giving nutrients that it gives out in its natural state. This nutrient is available all the time in the atmosphere and can be acquired by everybody who knows how to extract it when you are breathing. We can store so much of it up in our being for better use, but that is drifting away from the issue. The essential life-giving properties of Aether are evident to all people who are keen gardeners and who notice, that after a thunder storm, they can observe rapid growth in all the flora and fauna around in their gardens and in the general wildlife, too. You can observe that after a dry spell no matter how often you water your garden the plants become stunted to a certain degree, but once you get the natural rain, things greatly improve. But when the rain is highly charged when accompanied by lightning, the transformation is outstanding. Aether is one of the main life givers along with earth, water, heat, light and air. Aether is also referred to by many psychics and mediums as the etheric atmosphere, when they are detecting ghostly manifestations.

Now that I have set out the general gist of where electricity comes from and have likened it to water, we come to the movement and collection by the pumping method. If you need to transport water from one place to another, rather than take it by road tanker, you use a pump. It is placed in the main body of water to pump volumes of the stuff along a series of pipes or tubes to get it to where it is required, just like your water supply. It is the same type of principal with electricity and your electricity supply. All that a generator is is a type of pump for electricity, which it gathers up out of the atmosphere along with the positive and negative ions that go with it and then concentrates it down into powerful electricity. Then it is diverted and channelled along wires or cables, just the same as water is channelled when it is pumped along pipes or tubes to its destination. And the faster the dynamo gyrates, the more electricity or power it gathers. As long as the generator or dynamo is in the atmosphere when it is activated, it will pump electricity along the cables and wires to where you want it to go. And as long as either of these two (water or electricity) are confined and restricted we can control them, because once we have confined them to either wire or tube they are channelled to where we want them to go and be used. But if there are no wires or pipes connected to either of these pumps, although there is vast movement in both of them when the pumps are working, the product goes nowhere and both dissipate back into their own body from where they came from, with the loss, of course, of the energy used to work the pumps. We can store water in containers just like we can store electricity in containers (batteries). The two elements seem to love each other too, as they are always in close proximity in the atmosphere whenever there is a thunderstorm around. Uncontrolled electricity we know as lightning and the place lightning heads for is the ground. All electricity, whether static electricity, alternating current, or direct current, all wants to be grounded just like water does. This is because when it becomes condensed it is heavier than the atmosphere and falls, but in electricity's case it shoots rather than drops to the ground. It maybe just a coincidence, but the name of lightning carries part of the previously named lower vibration of light. Uncontrolled electricity also collects in pockets of static, similar to how water does when it collects into puddles, but differs from water this time by giving the unknowing victim a nasty shock when it uses them for a quick dash to earth through their body. If we could actually see how electricity collected and how it behaved (and this is the main point) in the same way that we can observe how water does, maybe we could do something spectacular with it, who knows?

But now that you have the general idea of electricity being like water, a fluid that flows and can be contained, why then can we not try to reinvent (dare I say it) the so called flying carpet, a vessel to float in electricity? We in our past lives knew of them, although they are now only in eastern fantasy stories. As bizarre as it may sound, you may one day in the near future be travelling just like it; this is a type of levitation and could be how levitation works, anyway. Levitation is a thing we don't understand, but we know it can be done and is talked about quite seriously these days. It may even have been the system used for carrying the stone blocks to build the pyramids, who knows? The pyramid builders, for instance, may have had the know-how of utilising the scattered particles of electricity here in our atmosphere to do just that, a form of antigravity. They certainly had the intelligence.

I will say no more on the subject, otherwise this work will solely be judged on this section alone and I, not being a scientist, cannot go any further other than to say: "to prove electricity is in the Earth's atmosphere continuously and we only generate it and do not make it we would have to ask NASA to test a generator or dynamo on the surface of the moon to see if it would produce electricity up there, like when they conducted that experiment for the gravity test without atmosphere using a feather and a stone. My money is on a generator being useless on the moon, producing no electricity at all, and solar panels being the only way to collect energy via the sun up there."

The next vibration up from electricity is the psychic force. We all have this force within us, but unfortunately it lies dormant in most all of us. The main reason for this is because most people are materialists and they pooh-pooh any form of phenomenon beyond their small limited minds; big brains, small minds. If their senses are inactive or dull and they fail to detect anything, then according to these insensitive people, whoever they may be, they will believe nothing else exists as far as they are concerned, other than what they can see or feel. That is their only outlook. Our western society, in all its glory I suppose, is at fault over this. After all, aren't we living in a physical, material world where we are supposed to gain all the physical experience we can while we are here so long as it harms no one and we don't break the rules? Our lives are governed by restrictions and it is how we are able to overcome and live with them as we planned our lessons to be, before we arrived back here, but only in the right way. This is how we progress and for those who are born with a so called silver spoon in their mouths, they have to overcome their illusion of superiority and accept that we are all the same without exception.

There are quite a few individuals who can utilise these psychic amenities within their human psyche and, in fact, we all posses them in some form or another. It's the not knowing they are there and that we have them at all that is the cause of our ignorance in this field. Persons who would like to activate these abilities will need to do some hard training to gain any psychic gift that lies dormant within their being. The controlling of one's scattered and uncontrolled thoughts would be a good place to start. The same laws govern the psychic world as govern the physical world in this matter. If you want to become an athlete, you have to train hard and practice. It is the same for a piano player who wants to play music, he has to learn and practice. And it is the same in whatever you do throughout your entire life, you don't get a free ride with anything unless you are very lucky or you have earned it.

Most of the psychic and metaphysical phenomena we are familiar with today is not generally acceptable to most of the scientists. However, we must all try to wean them away from their sceptical stance and somehow the two groups have got to work together. By doing so, we could and would find out and learn a lot more.

Our psychic senses do not belong to our physical senses; they belong to the spiritual side of things. Otherwise, we wouldn't know where we were. These senses only come into play when there is psychic phenomenon involved at times in our everyday lives, usually when we are quiet, relaxed, and our thoughts are of a higher vibration. During the hustle and bustle of the normal run of daily life, I'm afraid any sensitivity is lost to most any normal individual. So it becomes a major concern to any sensitive when things get really heavy and down to earth. You have to be in the right frame of mind to get anywhere.

This brings me to a very sensitive, but real, issue I have been delaying up until now because of the seemingly craziness of it and the unbelievably strange content it contains, especially to the materialist. But I am compelled, however, to include it in this book for the people of high sensitivity and who need this information for their peace of mind. In the previous article about electricity, I described how it acted in a similar manner to that of water. All sorts of life forms abound in water and if electricity has that likeness of water, then life is in electricity also, the same as we live in air. That is, of course, the uncondensed form of electricity called aether that is naturally present in the atmosphere. The problem we have is that we haven't the physical senses within us to see electricity or the uncondensed form of aether to detect what may live in it. Our senses are of a much lower frequency and they cannot pick up any of these higher vibrations, but a few people have and can detect this phenomenon. Those with psychic ability, which is a higher frequency than electricity, are without a doubt able to see these elementals if they try hard enough. I say this because there have been cases where some individuals have seen these nature spirits in the past, such as fairies, gnomes, leprechauns, pixies, elves, and goblins, etc. They are all different and all have been given names, but owing to the fear of ridicule it would bring onto the person who sees them in our modern world of today, no sightings would be or are reported. That is why most sightings are by children who are innocent and are oblivious of the ridicule they would receive if they were grownups. There have been stories told of sightings of these elementals at specific locations, usually around old tumulus or tumps (a small hillock or mound), sometimes at stone circles, circles of old Scottish pine trees, in the areas of outstanding natural beauty, most all junctions and crossroads of the lay-line grid that crisscrosses the United Kingdom, Ireland, and Europe, not to mention the rest of the world, and also in some areas of the national grid under the power line cables. An absurd statement to say the least, you may say, but there are things stranger than fiction and when we don't have the amenities to see these things, then how can we say either way whether they exist or not? It is a matter of choice for the individual. Funny how scientists can get away with talking about parallel worlds though, isn't it, and no one bats an eyelid. You will have to admit though, that there are thousands of fairy stories all going back into ancient times so who are we to judge?

The American Indians were sensitive enough to know that all life and living things had a spirit, all the way down to a blade of grass. They knew these spirits had to be respected. Any growing earthly object that is alive is only alive because it has a spirit force within it, but as soon as that force leaves that object, no matter how well or robust that object is or had been it becomes a dead object. It no longer exists and moves but instead breaks down

and rots away to soil and dust. How can it be said that there was-
n't a spirit in that object before it had died? We have become too
insensitive to realise how life needs a spirit to exist in the first
place and every living thing, no matter what it is, will fight to
live as long as it possibly can. Because it needs to fulfil, its task before it has to return to its source, that of old Mother Nature; in
some ways the spirit of the Earth. Every living creature values its
life as much as you value yours.

We forget so easily. We are never mindful for more than a few
moments when our consciousness is lost to us every night for
several hours. We don't know where we go or what we do for
those hours; all we do know is that our bodies have stayed where
they were from the time we go to sleep until the time we wake up
from our slumber. The body might as well be dead. But the body
can't die with the soul still connected to it, no matter what state
it's in because it's the spirit that is the life giving part, not the
body alone. The truth of the matter is that our outer casing, or
shell, that the vehicle of our soul resides in, and is technically
called a human body, is nothing more than a robot to us. We are
nothing more than robots with highly tuned sensors that trans-
mit the information they gather back to our spirit inside. This
may seem a bit like science fiction, but when you take a good
hard look, and I mean a really good and thinking, very hard look
at the way you work and how sophisticated and well thought out
your body is; it becomes more and more of an impossibility for
the case of physical evolution. Try as we may to find the answers
to our roots, it comes down to purely speculation and only speculation. Our bodies are of such a high technical and sophisticated
nature that none of us can figure out how the bloody hell we originated. And unless we change our way of thinking, we will never
in a million years find out the answer. Nobody even gives it a second thought; we take so much for granted. What we posses in
terms of the technology within us surpasses everything ever done
or invented. The thinking and planning of this soft machine we
call our body out does everything ever dreamed up or invented
on the physical plane and certainly was never conceived at first in
the third dimension. You may scoff, as most of us have done, at
the well known explanation dished out in the Bible, as many sci-

entists and scholars do now. The educated theorists have become the clever boys who have invented the evolution of the species theory because the ego of man can't stand the original story. But if you really give it some proper, deep thought, your conclusion must be the same as mine, that of awe and wonder. Somebody or something was very, very clever indeed. Not only to create a living machine, but to provide the material from the environment for it to be sustained the knowhow inside the machine for it to extract the right stuff so it can be sustained, and to give it the ability to reproduce itself. Isn't that absolutely amazing, a miracle in anybody's language. The story of Adam doesn't seem to be so farfetched if you refer to him as being the very first human body to be entirely composed and made up from the elements of the earth. Nowadays we are able to understand in a simplified way how our bodies are made up. Since the discovery of our DNA profile, the way of thinking I am putting to you doesn't come as such an unbelievable shock and we can basically go along with it.

At last, the temple of your soul has been rumbled and I mean this most seriously. You have to appreciate that this technical machine is quite capable of controlling you, yes controlling YOU. It has a built in auto-pilot and, in general, knows all your habits and ism's and can produce these characteristics at will. It should be able to; it came into being and has grown up with you since your return to the earth plane, and ever since that return you have been struggling to control it. Its biggest weapon against you is that it makes you think you are a brand new person, never before existing here. It makes you think it's your first time to exist here on earth and most everyone believes this because of the memory block. It is designed to supply you with any physical information you desire, but it usually pleases itself as we are unaware of our situation, having lost the sacred knowledge of how we work and what we are here for and that was long before the great flood. The other and main advantage it has over you is that your brain is brand-new coming with the new body, so it is always fighting in the egos corner; pushing the mind aside and forcing it to take a back seat, treating it as if it were only there for the ride. Because of this, it makes good reason for the mind not to feed the brain with its knowledge while the person's vibrations remain low and materialistic. Here lies the cause of so much bitter controversy between the physical world and the psychic world.

We should be able to regain control, as it cannot do without us. You are the spirit inside it that gives it life, but be very wary of what it can do. What you have got to remember is that it dies and you don't. It will cling to life and want many things, similar to that of the spoiled child who forever wants things. It always wants things that are usually bad for the soul and the worst struggle for the soul is when the body is young and virile. At this period of its life, it wants nothing more than to just reproduce. There is a built-in, highly active urge to guarantee continuation of life as it is in all species here on Earth, whether we like it or not, but this has been done on purpose. This built in mechanism has gone wrong and now doesn't work properly. The responsibility coordinates belonging to the emotions have weakened to an enormous degree and, in many ways; this has affected this urge and can change it into all sorts of uncontrolled violence. The search for quick thrills, regardless of the consequences, and then the desire to escape has become paramount. Hatred, greed, and jealousy are then produced within the violence and this causes any amount of untold damage to the poor afflicted soul inside the body. It brings on consequences for the loved ones outside, too. Responsibility is destroyed within the person who is the victim of these malfunctions and the damage done has to be paid for by this soul, regardless of its excuses. When your body becomes uncontrollable, the soul withdraws into a small section of your being. There it awaits the opportunity to regain control when some sort of quiet period comes along, usually during sleep, when the over soul (our link to the spirit world) gives out a strong rebuff and rollicking to the soul. The outcome for the person on the following day is depression. If the body is still in control and not the soul, it again seeks comfort in the same actions as caused its depression in the first place. The ego makes the body think the answer is to have more indulgences of the same thrill seeking action. So out he goes again, thrill seeking convinced it is the answer to his woes. So is the spiral downwards, and goes on down when the soul loses its control altogether. We have a responsibility to make sure this doesn't occur and this is done by remaining in some form of control, but really it is desired to be in complete control of what we want and what we do. Beware of temper and rage.

Alcohol is the opposite element of carbon. And it destroys our brain cells by the thousands and forces the soul out and away from the body, when you get intoxicated. You are also in grave danger of losing the ability to control your destiny. It may seem like fun to you or it may be escapism, but it is the worst course of action you could possibly take for losing it. Anything to do with the numbing down of the brain and senses is most damaging to the soul who is here to try and evolve. All actions made under the influence of induced drugs or alcohol for causing brain numbing trips, have to be accounted for and paid for by the individual who commits them, regardless of the circumstances. Loss of memory is no excuse if your body was the instigator, the onus is with you.

One of the oldest stories in the world was passed down by word of mouth every generation, for thousands of years, before it was written down. This was the crime of murder and was committed for the first time by Cain. This was such a shock to all of the people at that time, because they all knew why they were here on the earth. They knew that they were the soul conscious that was inside the body, learning about the material world and gathering knowledge for its own evolution, as well as for others. So why destroy a helpful machine and deprive a soul from his right to learning? It was so inconceivable and incredulous that such a horrendous crime could possibly be committed in those days that anyone then, wouldn't even have thought about ever doing such a thing. It was deemed so bad that all of his tribe were banished along with him. His people were all made to pay for his crime and since then we have slowly degenerated, having lost the very reason why we came here in the first place.

Man has been trying to regain complete control of his physical body for eons ever since then. There is much documentation, mainly of eastern origin, dating back centuries on similar themes of controlling the body, but our system in the west doesn't prescribe to that way of thinking. If it did, it would be misunderstood anyway because of the way we think here in the west. That is: controlling the body in the east means, controlling your actions, controlling the body in the west is to make it do things in a manual way, such as in athletics or some other sort of activity, a sort of sport or exercise where we can push the physical body to its limits to gain best of the bunch, so to speak, to gain a certificate to show that you have endured and pushed the body to its very limits, a show of will power to make the body go beyond its capability. Both meanings are controlling the body, but are totally different. The illusion is that we are in control because we can make the body do what we want, when we want, and how we want. Now isn't that just a brilliant illusion because the opposite is happening.

We don't see it because more than half the time the body does what we want for us anyway, but nobody believes that the body has gained control of the real you, the soul inside who has come back to attain for all the other missed chances in the past lives it lived. The body has become the big ego that now makes the decisions. It will throw its toys out of the pram when it can't get its own way, his or her vanity rules. In other words, the robots have taken over and are wreaking havoc on the earth. It is plain to see that if the soul was in charge there would be no horror in the world. The so called free will that has been granted to all of mankind has had its dire consequences, shown by what is happening in the world at large. Now it is for us all to try and sort out the mess, if we can, and we can all start with ourselves. We can try to set the proper example, as there is nothing anyone can do about the actions of our fellow soul travellers who have lost out to their egos.

You may be wondering if you are in control of your body rather than your ego. There is a very simple and subtle test to define this and that is: "have you been offended by anybody close to you and now are not speaking to them? Or, have you fallen out with a relation and decided never to speak to them again or anything in a similar vein?" If so, you have lost control. Only a balanced person, who takes no notice of such pettiness, can say they are in control, because the ego is proud and if that pride is in trouble, then it is offended; hence the rebuff. You can have pride in what you do, that's positive, but to be proud is egotistical and negative, which is the sign that you are not in control at all. The best remedy to cure being upset by somebody's remarks and therefore regain your control is to restart the relationship from before the fateful words or action took place. That which caused the rift in the first place should be rewound and you should revert back to how you were before the rift or split, when everything was okay. If you can't do this, then you have a problem with a large ego, to which you are going to have to subdue and then do a large amount of soul searching. Your efforts cannot be too small in this as it is the key to your progress. Here are the poisons the ego uses: rage, temper, lust, greed, gluttony, jealousy, envy, slothfulness, ambition, and pride, these are all the ego's weapons to defeat you in your quest to regain control. The virtues contained in your soul to help you regain control are: justice, prudence, temperance, courage, kindness, love, hope, faith, and intuition, along with a few more un-named righteous aspects, complete with a bucket full of humour. I believe anger to be neutral in this group, because how can you not be angry at someone's stupidity that causes hardship, suffering, pain, or even death?

It is a very slow process in gaining the wisdom required to free the soul from the rebirth cycle of reincarnation because all the pleasures and temptations put before us are designed to do just that. You just have to keep reminding yourself that your conscience is your guide throughout this life. And whatever you do will come back for you to pay for at the higher price later, because ask yourself, does the cost of living ever go down? So make sure you have no harming debts and you are, if possible, in credit to the good, and I don't mean with regards to money.

One question I would like you to ask yourself: if you had been educated as a child on the general material contained in this book, and if that were the case, I would presume it would have become the basis of your adult beliefs as our child education does this, so bearing that in mind, what would your reactions be if someone in authority suggested that we all originated from the sea, then we developed into apes and then changed from apes to our present form of human beings? Would you say, "You're having a laugh aren't you?" or would you consider it to be possible? Remember, what we are taught as children is what we believe. You now have to decide whether you believe what you were taught or need a re-think.

Hope this book has got you thinking, and just to start you off.

What came first the Chicken or the Egg?

This riddle can be answered, now you have read this book. It can be solved. After so many years of wondering whether this question could ever be answered, I can now answer it and state how it is possible. The chicken comes first and I arrive at my answer in this way:

Before you can start a production line for anything material, you have to have a prototype to base your production on, no matter what it is. Your first job is to make the prototype of what you want to make, in this case it is a chicken. Then you have to get it working. Once you have solved the problem of giving it a spirit for it to live (a very big problem yet to be solved), you then have to make, from your model an opposite for the work of creating the production line. After you have achieved this, you put all the frequency codes that contain the DNA genetics, the vibrating matter and all that makes up the parts from this material world, everything you used to make up your prototypes and put them into a specific set for production, which in the case of a chicken is the egg. There are many more complications to overcome before you can start to produce your finished item though, but the basics are there. Just a few technical adjustments and you are away, easy if you know how, mind blowing if you don't. I don't, we don't, because we are in a three-dimensional world but the theory is there, it just needs a higher consciousness to make it work.

If you look at all the animals, including man, living on the earth, they are all very similar in their make-up. This is no coincidence and is a multi-creational art form thought up by some intelligence which has a much stronger imaginative skill than the human brain. So once you have made one creature, you can vary your programme to make different models to suite your taste, (duck-billed-platypus) is a good example of mixing your animal blue print, which sure took some imagination. The only real problem is giving the models a spirit, and spirits as you know, come from a higher dimension, so you're stumped at the final outcome for getting any of them to work.

APPENDIX

During my search for information about my great-grandfather and the circumstances in which he was found, I was able to gather within myself a picture of an account that told me of some sort of cover-up by the family for fear of shame. There were two surviving members of the family from that time that I knew about, my uncle's wife, my Auntie Vi, and a second cousin living in America, my mother's cousin. I went to see my Auntie Vi, first to tell her of my experience and then to find out any information she could remember of the event. To my disappointment, she told me she knew nothing much about it because it happened two years before she met my uncle. But, there was one thing she remembered from when she got engaged to be married.

"Your grandmother," she told me. "Took me to one side and said that if Frank [my uncle] acts a little strange at times and seems rather withdrawn and touchy, it is because he found his grandad dead in the woods a few years ago and he's never gotten over it. He would get angry when we talked about it and say, 'you all don't understand about it, you weren't there and you should not talk about it like you do.' You see, his grandad had a rupture that he tried to cut out with a razor and killed himself doing it. And some of the family say he committed suicide. Frank doesn't like it when they talk this way on the subject, so now we don't talk about it at all. I am telling you so you know how it is and so, to be careful. And that really is all I can tell you my dear. Frank was a very private man and he never ever mentioned it."

I then managed to get the address of my cousin living in America. She was my mother's younger cousin so I suppose that would make her my second cousin. She was the youngest daughter of my great-grandfather's (or my), youngest son, Cecil Trigg. Who was the one who had the most to say at the inquest on his death? I wrote to her of my situation, calling her my aunt without thinking. I knew that the last time I saw her was when I was only four years old and wondered if she would remember me. Because of the content of my letter, I was anxious about whether I would get a reply or not (how sad is that, that you can't talk freely about reincarnation). Thankfully, she wrote back to me with this:

Dear Richard, sorry it took so long to reply. Received your letter and in answer to it, there is nothing I can tell you except that I was nine when grandad Trigg died, but when I grew up I was told by the family he had committed suicide the day they found him, but he was a wonderful man and everyone liked him in the village. He dealt with herbs and had a cure for everything, I loved him dearly, when my mother died we moved next to Gran and Grandad Trigg, I was just five then and they took care of us while dad worked. Your experience was really strange, I tried to find out as much as possible but my cousin told me what I have told you in this letter. However the day he died I didn't go with him, he always took me on walks usually gathering herbs to make something, and I vaguely remember he use to explain to me about plants. Hope this is of some help to you god bless, Auntie Grace.

These were the last two people I knew who had possible information on my great-grandad and what little they knew has helped me a little to reconstruct what transpired all those years ago. A picture has developed of what happened on that fateful day during the writing of this book. There is no doubt in my mind that I have been tutored while compiling it by the forces from beyond. Now there is an urge compelling me to divulge to you in this book of what happened so, to clear up the loose ends of this dramatic event, here are the final words of my story. You must remember at that time in 1935, there was no free hospital treatment available and no National Health Service, (N.H.S.).

There was a lump in my groin that was getting bigger and it had been concerning me for some months. It had started out from about the size of a pea and it had got to the size of a small egg, and was still growing. It seemed to be quite close to the surface of the skin, protruding outwards when I stood up and pressed against my clothes. I felt quite confident that I could cut it away if I could muster up enough courage to do so; to me, it would be no worse than having a tooth pulled. I kept this to myself, not wanting to alarm anyone. Besides, it was a personal matter occupying a personal place in my body. As you can imagine, the last two weeks of my life were occupied with these thoughts up until the final day.

On that typical November day, with the leaves falling from the trees in the wind, I set out for my usual walk. It was dull and chilly, and the idea was still in the back of my mind. As I walked I headed for the Beech Walks, one of my favourite places in the area, and spent a long time there, sitting under my usual large beech tree pondering over my dilemma. It seemed the right place for me in the quiet surroundings to consider again whether to go ahead with my plan. As I sat there, I grasped hold of the lump as I had done so many times before. And I thought I would only have to slice the skin across the surface of the lump and I could pop it out and be rid of it. Then I could hold the skin together for the blood to congeal and it would be the end of the thing for good.

I must have sat there for hours before I finally decided to cut it out. It would be quite simple, so after what seemed to be another hour I finally cut across the lump. Blood squirted out, but the lump didn't move. I put the razor back in my pocket and with both hands held behind the lump, I forced it out. The pain was hellish and the lump slipped from my grasp and fell into the leaf covered ground. I became alarmed at what I had done as I was losing blood, so I gripped my hand tight to hold the gash together. I realised I was in trouble, as it had left a big hole, and I needed to get some medical assistance quickly. I staggered up on my feet and made my way back towards the village. The light had started to fade and I had travelled about four hundred yards, cutting across the rough terrain to make a shortcut, when I became dizzy and fell over, wrenching my wound. I gasped with pain and got up again. By taking the shortcut I was not on the footpath. As I staggered a few more steps, I again collapsed with my head in a spin. The pain was acute and like a dull ache, and I could hardly bear it. I lay where I fell and pulled up my legs to ease the discomfort and rested. There I must have lost consciousness because the next thing I knew, I could hear my name being called out. But as I listened, the sound was getting farther away, fading in the distance. In desperation, I jumped up to call them back! Wow, this was such a strange feeling. It was pitch black and must have been well into the night, but I had no pain it felt as if I was floating. To my amazement, I was floating, I felt like the genie out of Aladdin's lamp; it seemed as if I was in a bubble and as I looked down I could see my curled up body on the ground. It was pulsating in time with the smoky connection leading to me and it gave me the sign that I was still alive, but was in a state of rapid deterioration.

I flew straight to my home to summon help. I tried to arouse my wife, but she would not respond to my gestures. It was if I was in a dream and I was invisible to her, she did not know I was there. I was panic stricken; I seemed to be in all of my families houses at the same time and the scenes I was observing made me more anxious. Everyone was acting like zombies in slow motion, full of gloom and doom. And the harder I tried to communicate, the more stressed I became. Time was running out. The only one to show any sign of response to me was my grandson, Frank. It seemed as if I was getting through to him. He was getting ready for bed and, as I was telling him where I was, he started to dress again. I urged him to hurry up, but then, he hesitated and sat down on the bed. My anguish was unbearable. I could read his thoughts; they appeared as pictures telling me he was thinking that he had already searched that area and it was just silly to go back out again so far into the night, but would be better to just check again in the morning.

My fate was sealed. I tried more communication, but to no avail. So I returned to my body and tried to get back into it; it was terrible, the cold and discomfort was a horrible feeling. I could not get back in properly; all that I had there before I left my body was gone. I could not move it; oh woe is me, what have I done? I didn't know then, but my anguish would be far worse later when I was found.

True to his thoughts, Frank set out from home soon after he awoke. It was late morning, since the late night search had caused him to sleep in. He went straight to where I was and his distress echoed through my being. I watched helplessly as his grief ran wild within him. He sat down beside me and we both wept together. I could not touch him. he didn't know I was with him. He was having guilty thoughts about not coming to get me when he had that feeling of knowing where I was and how he would never forgive himself. He was inconsolable. What have I done? How foolish I have been, I have burdened my wonderful grandson with my death and can do nothing about it.

He stayed by my side for what seemed like hours. Then came the sound of voices, he heard them, it was a search party lead by my youngest son Cecil. Frank called to them, "he's over here," and they came over to me, saw my body, and sent for the policeman. The last comment I heard was my son Cecil remark, "the silly old bugger's committed suicide,"

I often wondered why my Uncle Frank never had a good word to say about my Uncle Cecil when I was in his company as a boy, now I know why. But I must put on record that I myself was to blame for my dilemma. If I had not taken the action that I did, then I would have lived, although somehow fate was to play a major role in the outcome. This is not to say whether it is or was the right outcome, for as you can see the outcome is this book. There are forces that work in mysterious ways, their wonders to perform.

Frank went looking for me after he died, to find out what had happened, and found out I was back on Earth. I have felt his presence at times, while I have been writing this book, like he felt mine when I went to him on that fateful night to get his help as I lay dying in the woods. I have only one explanation to this and that is our sixth sense. So why don't we use it? He has helped me to complete this book; I have no doubt about that. What affect my death had on Frank only my auntie Vi and my three cousins would know and understand. I hope this will solve and settle any unusual trends of his attitude towards life that he had, if he had any of them at all. It is times like these that you come to realise that emotions rule our lives, emotions rule the world! Whatever you feed your emotions with, is what you get in the end, whether it be right or wrong, good or bad. Your passion is the strength of feeling that feeds the emotions with whatever you love or hate, therefore you must control your emotions. This is the key to your quest.

Authors note

The material and knowledge contained in this book is already known to everybody, but is not available to us without difficulty. It is all contained in the subconscious and the mind along with very much more. We have always existed and have had many lives. All of us have a huge problem in this material world when we return, manifesting in the makeup of first our brain insofar as it is new and contains no information whatsoever of our previous existence. And second, the educational part for that brain into the system you are born into controls your thinking. This is how and where you measure all the things you encounter. One problem will be whether to believe you have a spirit or not, and until you encounter someone's death you probably won't even consider it. How and when you come to this dilemma is how you will believe or not believe in life after death, it is as close as that. Unfortunately we are on our own in this matter unless we have been born to spiritually advanced parents and I do not mean religious fanatics but well balanced righteous people. Charles Darwin and Thomas Huxley are the men responsible for closing the door to spiritual growth in the west; they along with the creationists who follow the religious word without question have caused an, us and them syndrome. This causes an endless argument with no result of any value. I have introduced you to the alternative that was lost to mankind eons ago which contains some logic with no strings attached so that you can work it out for yourself. I wish you the very best on your journey and hope you have been blessed with the power of discrimination that you will need to attain your goal. One last comment, the ego hates quiet; it knows that when you are in a quiet state your vibrations are increased, this allows you to be able to receive information from your soul and from higher sources. If you must have constant noise for comfort, it might pay you to think again, it may just help you to learn something extra. Now is the time to start to re-read this book again so you can digest its contents a little more, or maybe it's not for you at all, the choice is yours, either way I wish you well in your physical life here. Yours truly Richard F Weaver.